M000200784

. . . **one of the most touching, beau**

When given a choice between seeking money and seeking wisdom, seek wisdom and you will have both. Money is simply the result of applying principles that create value in the lives of others and in the world. This book will be a beginning in your search.

—Jim Stovall, *President, Narrative Television Network*

Results of our survey of high school seniors' financial knowledge revealed a woefully below-average score of 50 percent. The results show that average graduates are entering adulthood unprepared to handle the complex financial world they will confront. Books such as *Wisdom Daddy Taught Me* can help to prepare young adults in basic money-management principles that many are not receiving in our nation's schools.

—Dara Duguay, *Executive Director*
Jump$tart Coalition for Personal Financial Literacy

This book is for everyone who truly loves their children. I've even given Suzanne a new name—Money Mom.

—Jeff Crilley, *Fox News, Dallas*

Filled with warmth, humor and love, *Wisdom Daddy Taught Me* gently leads readers to develop a prosperity consciousness that can change lives. An easy read and a wonderfully inspiring alternative to traditional financial how-to books!

—Gerri Detweiler
Author, *The Ultimate Credit Handbook* and *Slash Your Debt*

Suzanne's book has many practical and down-to-earth solutions to basic financial concepts, with childhood experiences that will make you nostalgic for a time when life seemed much simpler. The lessons are as applicable to today's youth as they were then. You will enjoy it.

—Ed Douglas, *Chairman/CEO, Citizens Bank & Trust Company,*
Chillicothe, Missouri, Author, Making $1,000,000 with Only $2,000

Financial lessons taught through delightful, yet inspiring vignettes. Thoroughly enjoyable and thought-provoking read.

—Victoria Girdziunas, *President, No Magic, Inc.*

Suzanne's book contains keen insights of her Dad's wisdom and zeal for life. I invite you to read and reflect on the wonderful "tidbits" of helpful information and advice.

—Jim Caswell, *Vice President-Student Affairs, Southern Methodist University*

Wisdom
Daddy Taught Me

I wish you wisdom
and prosperity.

Suzanne

*The further backward
you look,
the further forward
you can see.*

—Winston Churchill, *British Prime Minister*

Wisdom Daddy Taught Me

A Path from Poverty to Prosperity

Suzanne Short

Brown Books Publishing Group

Wisdom Daddy Taught Me: A Path from Poverty to Prosperity
Copyright © 2002 Suzanne Short

All Scripture quotations, unless otherwise indicated, are taken from the HOLY BIBLE, NEW INTERNATIONAL VERSION®. NIV®. Copyright ©1973, 1978, 1984 by International Bible Society. Used by permission of Zondervan. All rights reserved.

Cover photo of Sam and Suzanne Potter.

For information, please contact Brown Books Publishing Group
16200 North Dallas Parkway, Suite 225, Dallas, Texas 75248
972-381-0009   www.brownbooks.com

First Printing, 2002
ISBN 0-9719689-0-X
LCCN 2002091687

Printed and bound in the United States of America
10 9 8 7 6 5 4 3 2 1

Dedication

This book is dedicated to my children Kristina Kay, Suzanne Pauline, Joanna Nicol, and all my grandchildren. This book is an acknowledgment that Jesus Christ, my Lord and Savior, has blessed my life. To my husband, Bill, who supported and believed in me, and my wonderful brother, Sam, who is a vital part of my life, I hope this effort blesses you as well.

Contents

How We Survive and Thrive: Money

Acknowledgments

I want to thank and acknowledge the wonderful team at Brown Books who guided me through the publishing process. Milli Brown, whose enthusiasm for all her authors gives her an unmatched zest for the mentoring she provides. Kathryn Grant, whose editorial oversight is calm, certain, and reassuring. Kathryn's dry wit adds a great element of fun to such an elegant and competent lady. Suzanna Brown and Alyson Alexander, who handled the layout and cover design, were sensitive to each and every emotional link to the material. Without their creative talent I would have been truly lost.

I appreciate the many proofreaders who labored over my less than perfect punctuation. To the one who said she loved my father— thanks, Debbie Hansen.

I want to give extra recognition to a dear friend, Frank Seay, who actually took his precious time to read my very raw first draft. Without his enthusiasm for my project and his helpful suggestions I would still be in rewrites.

While all my children are wonderful, I would be remiss, if I did not acknowledge the extra effort and useful editorial comments I received from my oldest daughter, Kristy Russell.

I am indebted to Pastor Andrew McQuitty of Irving Bible Church, whose sermon on Matthew 25:14, *The Parable of the Three Talents*, confirmed for me that this book was meant to have a wider audience than my family. A grateful thank you to my former minister, Pastor Keith Stewart, whose spiritual leadership had a positive impact on my life.

Above all else, I wish to credit the Lord God for the gift of two wonderful parents and His guidance in sharing the wisdom that He gave Sam "Honey" Potter. I came to know that it was my job to share it with each of you.

Kick up your heels
and enjoy
Daddy's Wisdom

From Daddy's Girl

Introduction

I began this book for my children and grandchildren so that future generations might benefit from the wisdom Dad clearly possessed. As I began the task of writing, I recognized that Dad's wisdom should be shared with a larger audience.

From 1965 until 1981, I was a stay-at-home mom. In 1981, on my fortieth birthday, I reentered the job market in Tampa, Florida, as a Realtor. The '81 housing market was a nightmare. Interest rates were 17.5 percent. If you couldn't finance it, you couldn't sell it. I was a newcomer to Tampa, a relocation wife, with no friends and little knowledge of the schools or the city streets. I couldn't find the real estate, much less sell it. Through sheer determination, I prospered nonetheless.

By 1984, through a corporate family move, I started working as a Merrill Lynch stockbroker in Cleveland, Ohio. On January 29, 1986, my youngest daughter, Nikki, turned sixteen and on the same day my seventy-five-year-old father, Sam Potter, died in Dallas, Texas. I was forty-four, married with three daughters, and I had been back in the work force for less than five years. Dad's death was the first in a chain of events that would quickly change my life.

Within six months, I was back in Dallas for good and ensnared in a long and difficult divorce. I changed careers again and became a mortgage broker.

It was after Daddy's death that his role as my parent began all over again. My childhood memories of his teachings helped me build a financial strategy for my life as a single woman. As I worked year after year to rebuild my net worth, my father's words, mostly proverbs and adages of the 1940s and '50s, became my subconscious primer. Dad's sayings from the past were parenting me once again. His words were sound bites from my childhood; I remembered them and learned from his favorite phrases.

As I saw the financial light at the end of the tunnel, my vision expanded. I had viewed thousands of personal financial statements since 1981. I knew most people in our society were not doing what I was doing, and what they were doing did not work. Daddy's wisdom was a gift from God, and I knew it was my responsibility to share that gift.

This is a book about parenting and conditioning. It illustrates how one parent with very limited time can exert a strong and positive influence on a child. You will be able to see how my dad, Sam Potter, created an instructive and encouraging environment for his children. This book shows how an environment can be created to influence the development of a child. As the child in this book, through my eyes the reader will experience some of Daddy's lessons. The conclusions that come from the book reflect my thought processes, my interpretation of the instruction provided by my dad. I bring the hereditary side to the equation. As a child and as an adult, my thought processes are distinctly mine. They are my God-given thoughts and my God-controlled heredity. *Wisdom Daddy Taught Me: A Path from Poverty to Prosperity* will allow the reader to view the interplay between heredity and environment on three main topics that were the focal points of my dad's parenting: character, attitude, and money.

I was grounded in the fundamentals of strong character early on. The principles of honesty, commitment, and respect for others were themes of my dad's instruction. Reading the business headlines from any major newspaper in America validates that those who ignore these basic laws do so at their own ultimate peril. My dad's teachings on attitude can be found in every self-help seminar and published self-help book. Wisdom is not new; it is centuries old.

Financially successful people embrace, understand, and utilize the money concepts Daddy taught me. The life-value system in character, attitude, and money provides the skeletal tool set to build a productive life. These are only tools, as with all tools, they must be used and expanded to build anything of merit.

When *The Millionaire Next Door*, written by Thomas J. Stanley, Ph.D., and William D. Danko, Ph.D., was published, I had no interest in reading it. I knew instinctively what it would say. My friends repeatedly recommended the book. Finally, curiosity won out and I read it. It is a superb book, and it validated what I had long suspected. My dad was the prototypical millionaire next door!

I learned financial wisdom from a self-made, nonpretentious American millionaire! Although I suspected that my father might have accumulated a significant net worth, it wasn't until he died in 1986 that I really understood how amazing he was. The financial expertise he possessed was self-taught and self-executed. At his death, Dad held dozens of very small real estate notes, and each one was accurately posted and amortized by hand, the old-fashioned way. I have included a short biography of his life for the reader at the end of the book.

My mother was my dad's polar opposite. She never wanted to take the effort to learn financial things. In her opinion, that was "what Dad was for." Mom had never posted a check, much less balanced a checkbook, but that is another book with different lessons.

Fortunately, I was my father's daughter. He taught me the importance of self-reliance and financial responsibility. After Dad passed away, I helped my mother determine valuations for the required estate filings. I then learned that my father had lived off of his savings and investments for more than a decade and a half in retirement. He navigated the financial ravages of the inflationary '70s and early '80s and came out the other side still a millionaire. Mom was left with a net worth in excess of a million dollars and no debts whatsoever.

Mom outlived Dad by more than a decade and did not die in financial need, but sometimes it was not for the lack of trying. The contrast between Mom and Dad was inevitable. Mom encountered financial difficulty because she did not understand money or how to manage it. She was full of fear. She lost much. Many, many people took financial advantage of her vulnerability. She understood the loss of the tangible things that were physically stolen or "just walked out of the house." The paper assets that evaporated were never missed because she never monitored them. She did not understand. Those who could, manipulated her ignorance and created the losses.

I was grateful every day, as I struggled to keep Mom protected, that I had the financial background and inspiration from my father. Dad knew I would take over where he left off. I am sure that he had no idea how hard that would be.

Whether you are a man or a woman, I hope you enjoy my book. If you are a woman who would rather not worry about financial things, get a grip, girl! You are only delaying the inevitable. Start to learn now. Financial understanding is more vital today than it has ever been. It is an important life skill that knows no gender. Just dig in with the rest of us. Learn we must. If I can do it, you can do it.

Wisdom is the foundation of Wealth.
Wisdom is developed over time
and is an ongoing process.

–Affirmations of Wealth, V. John Alexandrov

THE WISDOM BEGINS:

A Letter from Father to Son

Sam Potter to His Young Son, Sam Potter, Jr.

Father Forgets

Sam Potter to His Young Son, Sam Potter, Jr.

*L*isten son: I am saying this as you lie asleep, one little paw crumpled under your cheek, and the blond curls stickily wet on your damp forehead. I have stolen into your room alone. Just a few minutes ago, as I sat reading my paper in the library, a stifling wave of remorse swept over me. Guiltily I came to your bedside—

These are the things I was thinking, son: I had been cross to you. I scolded you as you were dressing for school because you gave your face merely a dab with a towel. I took you to task for not cleaning your shoes. I called out angrily when you threw some of your things on the floor.

At breakfast I found fault, too. You spilled things; you gulped down your food. You put your elbows on the table. You spread butter too thick on your bread. As you started off to play and I made for my train, you turned and waved a hand and called, "Goodbye, Daddy" and I frowned, and said in reply, "Hold your shoulders back!"

Then it began all over again in the late afternoon. As I came up the road, I spied you, down on your knees playing marbles. There were holes in your stockings. I humiliated you before your boy friends by marching you ahead of me to the house. Stockings were expensive and if you had to buy them you would be more careful!

Imagine that, son, from a father.

Do you remember later when I was reading in the library how you came in, timidly, with a sort of hurt look in your eyes? When I glanced up over my paper, impatient at the interruption, you hesitated at the door. "What is it you want?" I snapped. You said nothing but ran across in one tempestuous plunge, and threw your arms around my neck and kissed me, and your small arms tightened with affection that God had set blooming in your heart and which even neglect could not wither. And then you were gone, pattering up the stairs.

Well, son, it was shortly afterwards that my paper slipped from my hands and a terrible sickening fear came over me. What has habit been doing to me? The habit of finding fault, of reprimanding—this was my reward to you for being a boy. It was not that I did not love you; it was that I expected too much of youth. I was measuring you by the yardstick of my own years.

And there was so much that was fine and good and true in your character. The little heart of you was as big as the dawn over the wide hills. This was shown by your impulse to rush in and kiss me goodnight.

Nothing else matters tonight, son. I have come to your bedside in the darkness, and I have knelt there ashamed!

It is a feeble atonement; I know you would not understand these things if I told them to you during your waking hours. But tomorrow I will be a real daddy! I will chum with you, and suffer when you suffer, and laugh when you laugh. I will bite my tongue when impatient words come. I will keep saying, as if it were a ritual: "He is nothing but a boy—a little boy!" I am afraid I have visualized you as a man. Yet, as I see you now, son, crumpled and wearing your cap, I see that you are still a baby.

Yesterday you were in your mother's arms, your head on her shoulder. I have asked too much, too much—

ABOUT "FATHER FORGETS": Written in the '40s. I found "Father Forgets" October 26, 2001, while writing *Wisdom Daddy Taught Me*. This letter had never been seen by his children. Dad clearly grew as a parent because I cannot remember one day with Dad that I did not laugh. Dad's eulogy at the end of the book shows the evolution of a loving man.

Author's Note

After the first edition of *Wisdom Daddy Taught Me* was printed, bound and in distribution, I discovered that I had inadvertently and mistakenly attributed the letter titled "Father Forgets," on pages 3 and 4, to my father. I found my dad's letter while writing this book. I assumed that my father had written it. I have now discovered the letter was originally written by W. Livingston Larned in the early 1900s, first published as an editorial under the title "A Father Forgets" in *Peoples Home Journal*, and subsequently re-printed over the years in hundreds of magazines, newspapers and books, including *Reader's Digest* and Dale Carnegie's *How to Win Friends and Influence People*.

Apparently, my father was one of many appreciative readers who hand copied the letter and saved it. He took the liberty of changing the last line from "…crumpled and weary in your cot…" to "….crumpled and wearing your cap," referencing a favorite cap of my brothers. My brother was so attached to the cap that he even wore it to bed. It was the reference to my brother's cap that convinced me that my father had written the letter. The misattribution will be corrected in future printings of this book.

. . . "richness" is at least as much a matter of character, of philosophy, outlook and attitude, as it is of money. The "millionaire mentality" is not . . . merely an accumulative mentality.

–J. Paul Getty

Who We Are:
Character

So in everything, do unto others

what you would have them do to you,

for this sums up the Law and the Prophets.

–Matthew 7:12

Remember the Golden Rule
A Guideline for Life

"You're hurting my chicken. Put it down!" I was so upset I was crying.

"I will not." She glared back.

I could see my big black chicken flapping its wings, trying to break free of Janis Sue Wynn's viselike grip around its neck. Dad and Mom raised a few chickens in the backyard. Janis Sue Wynn had caught a big black hen around the neck, and she would not let it go.

"Janis Sue, let my chicken go or you'll be sorry!" I bellowed.

"It's my chicken!" she proclaimed, tightening her grip.

Now I was about as determined as any four-year-old can be. I stamped my foot and said, "I'll fix you!"

As I raced inside the house, I already knew what I had to do. I had to get Janis Sue to drop my chicken before she strangled it. I was going to protect my chicken! I went straight to Mom's room and found a big diaper pin that belonged to my baby brother, Sammy Junior.

Out I raced, straight for the backyard.

"Put my chicken down, Janis Sue, or I'll stick you with this pin."

"You better not!" she screamed. So I stuck her.

The best that can be said is that she dropped the chicken. The worst was that I was not the least bit sorry I had stuck her. She ran home, screaming at the top of her lungs and rubbing her little three-year-old arm wounded with the diaper pin.

Gratified that my property had been reclaimed safely, I went into the house. But this episode was far from over.

Maydee, Janis Sue's mom, must have talked to my mom about what happened because Mom found out. I got a serious switching with a green peach tree limb.

Wow! If you've never had a switching, then you won't understand. Nothing, but nothing, stings quite like a switching with a peach tree limb. At four, I learned a very important lesson. The peach tree got my attention focused and made me a quick study.

Mom wanted to be sure that I got a slight dose of my own medicine. Hurting someone was not acceptable behavior! Inflicting a little pain to teach a child not to inflict a different kind of pain seems harsh these days. Perhaps. But I can only attest that the discipline worked. I would not have to relearn this lesson.

As I cried, I said I was sorry I hurt Janis Sue.

Mom said, "I'm going to have to tell your dad when he comes home. You could have really injured Janis Sue with that diaper pin. Suzanne, you have to have more respect for others, even if they are doing wrong. Two wrongs don't ever make a right."

I didn't remember getting into trouble like this before, and I was not looking forward to Dad being upset with me. I was only trying to save my chicken.

Later the next day, Dad came in for the weekend. I was outside on the big cement back porch when Dad came out and sat down beside me. Dad had an open diaper pin in his hand.

"Mom says you stuck Janis Sue with this big old safety pin yesterday. Is that true, Sissy?"

"Yes, Daddy. She was hurting my chicken."

"I know all about the chicken, Sissy. I want you to touch the point of this pin. You need to see how sharp this is. Go real slow and just barely touch it, be very careful."

"It's pretty sharp," he continued, as I shook my head and began to cry. "Don't you think if you got stuck with that pin that it would really, really hurt?"

"Yes, sir," I muttered, ashamed.

"You can't hurt other people to solve a problem. Two wrongs never make a right. You must learn to use your head and come up with other solutions. If you are not sure that you can solve a problem without hurting someone, do nothing until you get good help to think through your options. Do you understand what I'm telling you?"

"Yes, Daddy, I should have gone to Mom and told her."

"That's right, Sissy. Even when you deal with people who act badly, always ask yourself: Would I like it if someone treated me the way I am treating them? If the answer is that you wouldn't like it, then don't do it! If you live by the Golden Rule, you can't go wrong."

The memories of many decades float together in time. In the haze, time becomes blurred, but the individual thoughts remain clear. From my earliest memories to this day, I knew that my father was a man clearly centered in an ethical structure that followed very closely the biblical rules for life.

For Dad, things were black or white. A choice was right or it was wrong. There was very little gray in his decision-making process.

Today, society seems lost in a sea of gray. The society of the '40s and '50s did not share the same ambivalence. Contemporary versions of right and wrong have become situational. Wrong choices have a thousand justifications. How difficult it must be for a child to find a moral center. Media escalates the mixed signals; good is cloaked in evil and evil is cloaked as good.

You and I live in troubled times. Too few children and too few adults have experienced unconditional love from a parent. God gave me not one but two parents who gave me unconditional love. The benefits of that are impossible to measure.

The Golden Rule was Dad's central rule of life. He made it clear that the Golden Rule was the cornerstone of character. The first and strongest lesson my father taught was the lesson of character. He taught me to give the other person the benefit of the doubt. I learned to treat others the way I wanted to be treated.

GUIDELINE FOR LIFE: The second most important commandment given by Jesus in the *New Testament* is: "Love your neighbor as yourself." (Mark 12:31) All the lessons of character can be found in Scripture, and the fundamental rule for living with your fellow man is the Golden Rule.

When Beggars die, there are no comets seen;
The heavens themselves
blaze forth the Death of Princes.

–Shakespeare

Don't Kick a Man When He's Down

Self-Superiority

*E*very now and then, when times were quiet, Dad and I found ourselves alone at the kitchen table. Sometimes, Dad would reflect on the wisdom he had gained by living through the Great Depression.

You might think that Dad was prone to long dialogues and interesting stories about the "old days." Sadly, that was not the case. In fact, Dad never disclosed anything about his family and little information about his youth.

The main way Dad shared his wisdom was to offer his simple observation or conclusion. Dad would lean over his newspaper and cup of coffee and say, "Sissy, life can take some surprising turns. Good people can find themselves down and out of work. Just remember— Never kick a man when he's down!"

It was as though something in the newspaper had triggered a memory that forced Dad to adopt the mode of teacher, however brief the moment.

After such a pronouncement, he would often change the mood by getting up to fill his coffee cup, leaving my childhood brain to store the memory of his words for later use.

Dad assumed that we, even as children, had the capacity to comprehend and implement his abbreviated advice. When I think back, I wonder if Dad felt that long, sentimental stories were too preachy, or if he felt the lessons were so deep that they would touch a resonant chord too sensitive for him to explore.

Neither Sammy Junior nor I asked many questions, which now seems odd. I always felt that questions about Dad's family were in areas that were private to him, and the answers were in places he did not want to go. Dad did not believe in living in the past. He chose to live in the present, while he maintained a plan for the future.

During the Depression, the economic fate of many families changed almost overnight. My dad believed in helping a friend when he was down on his luck. I can remember Mom mentioning to us kids that Dad had helped a customer adopt an Indian child. Later, she would tell us he had lent many of his customers the funds to start their own store or provided them with bridge financing during hard times.

These memories left me with a sense of vulnerability and an awareness that many things in life are outside our control. There are many ways to be in a lesser state. Not all of them are economic.

How many times have we seen someone picked on because they were different? How sad that is. But for the grace of God, that person could be one of us, and then where would our superiority and arrogance reside? It is an offense to our Creator to ridicule a fellow creature. Kindness and compassion are always the order of the day.

SELF-SUPERIORITY: Integrity without compassion is empty, and character based only on self-interest is not character. "Each of you should look not only to your own interest, but also to the interests of others." Philippians 2:4

Beauty Is Only Skin Deep

Beauty

*D*on't you just hate the term "pleasingly plump"? Plump is only pleasing to parents. No one, other than Mom and Dad, seemed to believe that plump is pleasing! I don't know what country you're from, but in the USA "pleasingly plump" is an oxymoron. You can be plump. You can be pleasing. You cannot be both! I spent too many years, from age eight through age eighteen, in a chronic state called "pleasingly plump."

Dad tried to reassure me about my overweight condition. Soon, I began to discount what he said, because, of course, I knew better. I knew Dad was just trying to soothe my damaged self-image. His viewpoint was clearly biased and blinded by fatherly love.

The first time I overheard Dad say that "beauty is only skin deep," I didn't grasp his meaning. I thought if you were beautiful, you didn't care how deep it was. I missed his point. Perhaps I just refused to see the real point. I wanted what other girls had—inner and outer beauty. Boys didn't care about all that inner beauty. Given a choice, a guy was always going to look for the "pretty girl." I was convinced that Dad only used this adage to make me feel better.

I'm sure that many times Dad did use this saying for just that reason. I also assumed that this adage only applied to the feminine gender. Isn't it amazing how preconceived ideas and assumptions get in the way of our understanding?

Society's addiction to beauty has multiplied a thousandfold since I was a girl. The pressure for the perfect look is omnipresent. Physical beauty makes a woman feel valued in our society. Lack of physical beauty leaves us groping for significance and meaning.

The movie stars of the '40s and '50s were totally captivating. When I was a child, only a very few women bothered with makeup. Most American women had no idea how to capture the glamour of the movie queens. Movie stars were outrageously beautiful, and they dressed in the kinds of clothes that were never seen off the silver screen. Some of my earliest memories were of the beautiful women from the movies. Their hair was beautiful, their figures perfect, their clothes breathtaking. The glamour of their lives was beyond anything a young girl could imagine. Movie stars gave us the image we dreamed about. Movie stars were our magic—our fantasyland.

I also admired the pretty girls in school. I went from envy of Billie in third grade to envy of Joanna in junior high school. My early lessons on personal gratitude slipped far away into my memory. I continued to wish for what I did not have.

Anytime I mentioned how beautiful or pretty someone else was, my mom or dad would chime in: "Beauty is only skin deep" or "Pretty is as pretty does." No further explanation was given, and I never believed it. I was not able to appreciate the wisdom of their words.

Over time, I did get it. As I matured, I began to understand that a beautiful figure and face means very little if it is wrapped around a mean spirit. Face and figure cover the inner person only for a short time. When the soul is ugly, no face or figure can hide it for long. Physical beauty attracts but it does not sustain. It will not sustain a job, a marriage, or a friendship. Male or female, this truth applies.

BEAUTY: The value of true beauty is found in the beauty of character. Our character has the ability to transcend our lifetime. Joan of Arc and Mother Teresa had beauty of character and will still be admired on this earth long after you and I have ceased to exist. Real beauty is internal and eternal.

Men often become what they believe themselves to be.
If I can believe I cannot do something,
it makes me incapable of doing it.
But when I believe I can, then I acquire the ability to do it,
even if I didn't have it in the beginning.

–Mohandas Gandhi

Watch Out for the Ugly Duckling

Evolution

Sam Potter was not a handsome man. He knew it, and he didn't seem to care. He was bald. He was short and fat. He wore glasses, and he had a very big nose. The most discouraging thing anyone could tell me, his daughter, was that I looked like him. Dad knew that I would rather look like Mom, because she was really beautiful.

I remember Dad teasing when someone brought up the fact that I looked like him as a baby: "Yeah, Sissy, don't you want to grow up and look like me?" And to really bait me, he would add the kicker, "When I was a kid, I was an ugly duckling but just look how pretty I turned out!"

It was a good thing that I was used to Dad's teasing; otherwise, I might have been tempted to cry. As he finished, he said, "There's a lot of truth to the story of *The Ugly Duckling*, Suzie. I've seen it over and over again all my life. You need to watch out for the ugly duckling. They'll fool you every time."

Dad believed in what he was saying. I'd seen him spot an unattractive child and predict that he or she would grow up to be a visually striking adult. If you felt that you were an ugly duckling, as I frequently did, Dad's words gave you hope. Dad enjoyed kids. He loved their funny and fresh perspective. He enjoyed watching the evolution of the child into the adult, and he relished being a positive force in that transition.

Dad had a good friend, Bill Potts, who had four daughters. All of the girls were very different in their hair color and skin tone. Trisha was the third born and was teased unmercifully by her older sisters about her easily sunburned fair and freckled skin. Dad told his friend outright, "Billy, you mark my words, little freckled-face Trisha is going to grow up, and she'll be a knockout. Just you wait and see. She'll put her sisters to shame."

Trisha was a skinny, redheaded, pale, freckle-faced little girl. At age nine, Trisha was clearly no comparison to her three pretty sisters. Trisha was skinny with an awkward, scrawny frame. Trisha was so fair-skinned that she had to wear a big hat and long-sleeved shirts to protect her skin from the blistering Texas sun. No one else saw the beautiful woman that Dad saw!

Dad looked into the future and envisioned a strikingly beautiful auburn-haired beauty. Dad saw another Rita Hayworth or a gracious Maureen O'Hara. Dad told Trisha not to let her sister's teasing about her floppy sun hats and fair, freckled skin hurt her feelings. He said, "One day they will want to look just like you. You're going to outshine them for sure!"

Dad painted a future vision and encouraged Trisha to see herself as a beautiful grown woman with hair the color of a copper penny. And in his typical style, he would add, "those girls had better watch their hole card." In other words, Trisha would see the day when her sisters would wish they had the gifts she had received. My dad loved to help children find their sense of self-worth and the courage to look ahead into a changed future. Dad's compliment was totally sincere, and his vision was a stronger encouragement for Trisha than any story telling of *The Ugly Duckling*.

As a fat, little, twelve-year-old, I secretly felt that maybe there was hope for me, too, in the future. I did not have sisters who teased me, but I did have a brother who had labeled me "blubber puss."

I will never know whether Dad's story about Trisha was his double-edged sword. Could it have been his way to show both his own daughter and Trisha the beauty of tomorrow? Dad had the wisdom and the ability to show a child the swan within.

EVOLUTION: We are constantly changing and evolving mentally, emotionally, spiritually, and physically. Over time our physical presence changes and alters. The older we become, the more impact our inner-self has on the appearance of our outer-self. The graceful butterfly starts life as a caterpillar and the storybook swan from Hans Christian Andersen's book began life as an ugly duckling. Life transforms if we will exercise patience. "The present does not equal the future." Tony Robbins

What lies behind us and
what lies before us are small matters
to what lies within us.

–Ralph Waldo Emerson

Beauty Is in the Eye of the Beholder

Viewpoint and Tolerance

"Oh, no. Miss Alabama was the prettiest! How could they have picked someone else?" I couldn't believe my eyes and ears. How could the Miss America judges select anyone besides Miss Alabama?

Dad started to laugh at me. Now, I was getting angry.

"I don't think it is so funny, Daddy. Those judges are stupid. How could they pick Miss Maryland? It doesn't make any sense." I was fuming at what I thought was an unfair decision.

"Suzanne, you better learn something right now about life. Not everyone sees things the same way. And that goes for beauty as well as a hundred other things. Whether it is work or play or a beauty contest, what is appealing to one person is not always appealing to another. That's why for more years than I can remember, people have been saying that 'beauty is in the eye of the beholder.'"

The Miss America Pageant would be the first of many lessons on different points of view. At the time, I didn't understand what Dad meant. I thought everyone saw the same thing when they looked at someone. If what we saw was the same, then, I thought, we should reach the same conclusions.

It was many years before I connected the idea that what people saw probably was the same, but how individuals valued what they saw was different.

I left my thoughts on the beauty contest decades ago, only to re-examine points of view years after my father passed away. I was not a young girl anymore, bewildered by beauty pageants. I was a grown woman observing divisive groups in our society yell and shout accusations at one another over different solutions to national problems. The stakes were higher and more significant than a beauty pageant. We observe political and social problems; however, the conclusions we each draw and the solutions we offer are filtered through our own unique value system and point of view. The very nature of our unique humanity cannot help but lead us down the path of personal interpretation. Our own opinions dominate and few of us are willing to see beauty in the opinions of another.

Fifty years ago, I thought one girl in a Miss America contest was clearly the one who should win. Daddy told me that it was only my opinion. He taught me to acknowledge the fact that the judges thought another girl was more deserving. I think of his words when political differences flare and opinions clash. I only hope that those with a different vision from mine will continue to grant me the space to hold a different view. This is an important American tradition called tolerance.

VIEWPOINT AND TOLERANCE: It is human to view life in our own unique way. Because of that, we place our own individual interpretation on what we see and hear. The strength of our country is that, as Americans, we have the right to hold our own points of view. In this free nation, each man has the right to draw different conclusions from the same information. There is beauty in the tolerance of different viewpoints. Two people of different views can both have character. It is not the same perspective that creates character, but how we handle our own point of view.

Wisdom is more precious than rubies,
and nothing can compare with her.

–Proverbs 8:11

A Penny for Your Thoughts

Value of Thought

I was just sitting, staring out into space when I heard Dad say, "A penny for your thoughts, little girl." How many times had I heard him ask that question? Even as a child, I knew it was just an invitation to open up. It was Dad's way of being there for us kids. Because Dad was on the road as a traveling salesman all but three weekends a month, I think he felt the time away left him missing the important pieces to really connect with our lives.

"I don't know, Daddy. I just was wondering what it would be like to be pretty and popular," I stammered.

"You are a pretty little girl. What makes you think you're not?"

"I don't know Daddy, I just know I'm not," was my reply.

"Well, you are pretty, and you'll always be beautiful to me. Even if you weren't pretty, there are more important things in life than just beauty. I'm not pretty and I'm having a good time." I laughed because Dad was not a handsome man and he knew it. And, he truly didn't care.

Then Dad got more serious than usual and said, "Pretty is often overrated. Pretty goes away with age. What one person thinks is pretty someone else does not. Anyway, if you go where you want, and you are with the people you enjoy and have the things you need, you can be very happy. It is possible to be pretty but not happy. Put that thought in your head, little girl, and you tell me what you would rather have?"

I knew Dad was right, but it didn't stop me from wanting both.

Since Dad died, I've often wondered why he used to say, "A penny for your thoughts." In some ways, he was letting me know that what I thought had value. He was indicating a willingness to trade value for value. By offering up a casual phrase, he left the willingness to share up to me, without pressure. Dad really wanted to help if I had a problem. His words were gentle and nonthreatening and gave no direction as to what he wanted from the dialogue. He was just there, ready to listen. Dad was always so logical and unemotional that he made life seem clear and simple.

If he were here today to ask me that question and to offer to pay me a penny for my thoughts, what a conversation we would have. My thoughts are that God gave me a gifted mentor whose lessons should be shared with others, and that is what I have chosen to do now. What I wouldn't give to hear his voice ask that question of me today. I would say, "Daddy, my thoughts are about you. My mind questions over and over again why was I chosen to be blessed with such wonderful parents."

VALUE OF THOUGHT: Our thoughts are our greatest source of value. Every created thing was a thought before it was a thing.

Straighten Up and Fly Right

Rules

" **S**traighten up and fly right," Sammy Junior and I chimed in with a giggle.

We had beaten Dad to the punch this time. Sammy Junior had been irritating me, while I was cutting out some paper dolls. For lack of a better idea, Sammy grabbed the paper doll and ran with it. The chase was on. As we raced round and round in smaller circles, Dad got up from his chair, and just as he opened his mouth, we both shouted his popular refrain. We both started to giggle and forgot the paper doll chase.

Whenever Sammy Junior or I misbehaved, Dad would very simply tell us to "straighten up and fly right." Anger was not an emotion that my dad enjoyed. So he was seldom angry. Dad preferred laughter; even his reprimand was fun in its firmness. I'm sure my brother and I gave Mom and Dad cause to lose their temper many times. Even though I recall getting a switching with the fine green limbs of a peach tree usually administered by Mom, I seldom saw Dad angry or mad.

A switch could really sting a little bare leg. It did not take many times of getting in trouble to learn that the straight and narrow was a better path than the one down to the peach tree.

As I got older, the only admonition needed was Dad saying, "Straighten up and fly right." I knew I was out of line, and I'd better get back in formation.

RULES: Character is both taught and developed. If children have been taught what is right, as they begin to accept the rules, then all that has to be done or said is to remind them that they know what to do and they need to just do it. If children are not taught correct behavior, it is folly to believe that a child will learn it independently. "Train a child in the way he should go, and when he is old he will not turn from it." Proverbs 22:6

Our virtues are most often
but our vices disguised.

–François duc de la Rochefoucauld

All That Glitters Is Not Gold

Fool's Gold

Sammy Junior was so excited that his small hands were literally shaking. Dad just stood back and watched with a clear sense of pride as Sammy Junior tore open the special delivery package. As he pulled the top off the box, he exposed the surprise gift, rocks for his rock collection. It seemed only moderately interesting to me. There were about thirty rock specimens pasted to a board and each rock was carefully labeled and identified. Most of the rocks looked ordinary to me, but one of the rocks, called pyrite, was quite pretty. It sparkled in the light and was so different from the rest of the ordinary offerings.

"What is pyrite, Daddy?" I asked with renewed interest.

"Pyrite is fool's gold, Suzie Q. In the California gold rush, a lot of old prospectors were fooled by this rock and thought they had discovered gold only to be later disappointed that it was worthless pyrite." Dad seemed glad that I was interested. Dad grinned and added, "All that glitters is not gold. More than just a few prospectors have been fooled by perceived value only to find out that real value was not there."

As a child, I thought there was very little chance that I would ever go looking for gold, so "all that glitters is not gold" was not an important warning for me. But life is full of exciting and colorful propositions. Dad's warning was that many things in life look much better than they really are. His caution to Sammy and me was to not get caught up chasing "fool's gold."

As I moved into my teens, I began to identify some of the things Dad was talking about. Teens frequently jump to conclusions. Some adults do the same thing. As a teen, I noticed how often popularity was based on appearance or prowess on the football field. The glitter was all that seemed to matter. In fairness, the "beautiful people" often were bright and kind human beings, but just as often, a teen's glitter obscured the fact that he or she behaved as a nasty individual. Many times, these glittering individuals would use the power of their popularity to abuse those who had not been blessed with the same exterior gifts. Power seemed to cloud judgment. Sometimes, a popular teen became more important in his own eyes than anyone else around him. The power of popularity can give a misdirected teen a license to be crude, mean, and abusive.

I began to unite two of Dad's sayings: "beauty is only skin deep" and "all that glitters is not gold." Bringing these two sayings together made it easier for me to understand when I was witnessing "fool's gold." I was intrigued that a number of my school friends did not share my observations. Excuses for the beautiful and popular people frequently flowed from the mouths of blinded admirers. Most students wanted to believe that the glitter was, in fact, gold.

The skill of discernment was easier for me because Dad had given me very simple tools. Dad's tools were simple to remember, and the "truths" could be broadly applied. "All that glitters is not gold" applies to buying a home, selecting a car, picking a job, finding a friend, or looking for a life-long mate. Another way of saying the same thing might be "don't let your eyes deceive you," or "never assume anything." It is ironic how many times in my life my brain recalled and used this particular caution from my dad.

Today, I see the same pattern among many adults, and it seems to me that it is reaching dangerous proportions. We seem to idolize, even as adults, the beautiful and popular people. The power and respect we give to idols is often not deserved. We do not want to let go of our desire for them to be real gold, even when they clearly cannot pass even the simplest quality "assay test."

We allow movie stars, sports figures, and politicians to set patterns of behavior through our adulation. Instead of holding the privilege of admiration for those who display honorable and desirable characteristics, we seem to no longer require that our role models exhibit the true gold of character. Our adulation endorses their bad behavior and misdirects our children. Celebrities seem to have the full reign of bad behavior with our endorsement.

Media seem to glorify extramarital sex. Children are born without the benefit of two committed partners (which is to say children's needs are secondary to the desires of their single parents). Movies depict teens and small children using language that should call for bars of soap to wash out their mouths. When these are accepted behaviors the glitter is dispelled, and the gold is nowhere in sight.

FOOLS GOLD: If you accept public opinion as your own, you may end up adopting principles and beliefs that will not support you or your family. Popular values are no substitute for thoughtful personal values. Each of us must evaluate the character of those we emulate, revere, and follow.

Reckless words pierce like a sword,
but the tongue of the wise brings healing.

–Proverbs 12:18

Don't Ever Say Anything You'll Regret

Verbal Responsibility

*H*aving a little brother was definitely an overrated experience!

Mom was always telling me how lucky I was to have a little brother to play with. She said that I "should be grateful because a lot of children don't have any brothers and sisters of their own."

For the life of me, I didn't see any benefits in having a little brother. Boys never wanted to play dress-up. They didn't like dolls. They thought bugs and snakes were fascinating and wonderful creatures, and the dirtier they could get and stay, the better. What they wore and how they smelled simply didn't matter. A sister might be okay, but there was absolutely no benefit in a brother!

Perhaps, Mom's opinion was clouded by her own wishful thinking. Mom had several half-sisters and half-brothers, but for most of her life she was brought up by her grandmother or her aunts. Mom never had a stable and long-term place to live. She was always someone's stepchild or half-sister. Mom longed for the complete connection that the very word "step" precluded.

It was a beautiful spring Sunday, and Mom and Dad were working in the backyard on Waco Street, cleaning up and burning the debris. Sammy Junior and I were playing in the big sandbox that Earl Dee, Dad's brother, had custom-built for our backyard. I brought out my favorite doll with her cream-and-pink velvet dress. Mom had made several more beautiful outfits for her, and I was eagerly changing her clothes. I was sitting on the edge of the sandbox in a pretend world that only a six-year-old can create. As I changed my doll from one lovely dress to another, Sammy Junior's boredom with the sandpile began to intensify.

At first, I just ignored his irritating sand tossing. Since his efforts were getting no response, he began to grab my doll's dresses and bury them in the sand.

He had stepped over the line! I screamed at Sammy Junior to stop. Just then he threw sand in my hair, and that was it! I punched him in the stomach and pushed him back down into the sand. His fanny hit the sand with a pop.

Sammy Junior started screaming and crying as I yelled out, "I hate you, Sammy Junior. You're going to ruin my doll. I wish you were dead!" Before I could think about what I had done, Sammy Junior jumped up crying and ran straight to Mom.

"What's the matter? What's the matter?" I could hear the concern in Mom's voice. She had no idea if he was hurt or not because she had been busy at the back of our lot.

"Are you all right? What's hurt?" she asked again, trying to get him to speak.

"Suzie hit me." Sammy Junior muttered.

Unlike Mom, Dad heard the whole thing and was headed at a fast clip toward Sammy Junior.

By then I was running to Mom, crying and trying to plead my case. I felt that I had been justified, and I didn't want to get in trouble.

I immediately heard Dad say in a very stern tone, "Suzanne Potter, did I hear you say that you wished your little brother was **d e a d**?"

Before I could respond to what was going to be a pretty stern lecture, Sammy Junior ran around behind Dad and grabbed his leg and yelled out, "No, no, Daddy she doesn't want me dead! She wants to kill me H E R S E L F!"

Dad did a double take at Sammy Junior's exaggeration and doubled over in laughter. The exaggeration was such a surprise that Dad couldn't contain his laughter. By this time, Mom was trying desperately to keep from smiling. When Dad quit laughing at the foolishness of the situation, he began to "straighten me out."

"Sissy, I know that Sammy Junior is no angel and that he was baiting you, but you are plenty big enough to come to one of us to settle the problem. But the real problem here isn't that you punched and pushed your little brother. We can resolve that. But the things you said and wished for can be dangerous! What if something did happen to someone you said that to? You would feel bad about it all your life. You would feel bad forever. But more important than anything else, you need to learn to "never say anything you'll regret.""

Dad was right.

Words can be more hurtful than deeds. Words never go away. They replay in the brain over and over again with equal or greater power to hurt. A physical hurt or injury usually hurts only a short while. The pain may be intense initially, but it dissipates. When we reflect on or attempt to relive the physical injury, it seems to replay without the physical sensation of the relived pain. But hurtful words are emotionally anchored to the emotional pain. We cannot recall hurtful words without reliving the emotional pain.

"Don't ever say anything you'll regret" goes beyond good advice. The words are wise. Dad counseled us to control our hurtful tongues. Our words, as well as our deeds, were our individual responsibility.

Without the restraint to hold our tongue, a marriage can be devastated by hateful and thoughtless words. Families can be torn apart in such a way that nothing can mend the damage. Words can never be taken back. They remain in the mind. Time does not erase their damage.

Verbal Responsiblity: Words are powerful and should be selected with care. Words can cause both pain and pleasure. The spoken word has a lifespan long beyond the moment. Weigh your words with care. We need to be prudent with our words, eager to praise and slow to blame.

Children have never been good
at listening to their elders;
but they have never failed
to imitate them.

–James Baldwin

Hear No Evil, See No Evil, Speak No Evil

Behavior

I still remember the tiny, dark-brown ceramic no larger than three inches high by four inches wide. It was a figurine of three little monkeys. The first monkey held his hands over his ears, the second monkey held his hands over his eyes, and the third monkey held his hands over his mouth.

The monkeys' first admonition was, listen only to the good things about people. Assume the negative things said are a misperception either by yourself or another person. Second, look for the good aspects of every human being and overlook the shortcomings that show up. Third, hold a hurtful tongue and never speak badly of others or spread negative rumors. The message of the three monkeys sounds so simple, yet it is a hard standard to live by.

There was something cute and playful about the three monkeys. Or perhaps, it was just the humor in human-like behavior, covering their ears, eyes, and mouth with two furry hands. Dad giggled when he said the "gossips" had the hardest time of anybody with the wisdom taught by the three monkeys. "They just can't help letting their tongues wag."

How many times have you been hurt by someone who repeated something about you that was untrue? How many times have you been hurt by someone who saw something you did and misinterpreted your actions? And they chose to take the most negative view of your actions.

The most damaging action is to say something hateful, hurtful, or ridiculing. Hearing evil and seeing evil corrupts the mind, but speaking evil multiplies the spread of evil through hurtful words.

If we follow this advice, we will treat our fellowman better. We will also foster an attitude that we hope others will adopt toward us. Can you remember the hurtful tongues of your childhood? Did it take you hours, weeks, or years to recover from the sting of cutting or subtle criticism? Did someone belittle you only to elevate himself?

No one grows tall at the expense of another. "Hear no evil, see no evil, speak no evil," teaches a lesson even a monkey should follow.

BEHAVIOR: By repeating hurtful things, we set in motion injury to our fellowman. None of us attains perfection in this world, so why find fault in others? A person of character knows that there are enough faults needing remedy within ourselves to occupy us for a lifetime.

Be kind,
for everyone you meet
is fighting a hard battle.

–Plato

Sticks and Stones Will Break My Bones, but Words Will Never Hurt Me

Self-Esteem

$\mathcal{M}$y feelings were hurt beyond repair. As a fourth grade elementary school child, I had fallen victim to the unkind words of a young classmate. A little girl made fun of my clothes and said that I was fat. I had never given much thought to the clothes I wore to school. I just let Mom pick them out for me. From that day forward, I became more vigilant in the selection of what I wore.

I learned that "different" was not good; being different raised the need to be evaluated. It opened you up to public comment. This was the beginning of my conformity to popular dress. To this day, I remember that classmate's name, yet I don't recall the name of any other child in my fourth grade class.

I know the little girl who hurt me quickly forgot who I was and what she said to me that was so mean and hurtful. But in my mind, it is still a clear memory, unfazed by time.

When I arrived home from school, Dad could tell something was wrong by the look on my face. I must have wanted someone to notice so that I could find comfort and support. "What is the matter with you, Sissy? You look like you just lost your best friend," was Dad's reaction to my troubled face.

"One of the girls in my class said my culottes were dumb looking and made me look fat."

"Well," Dad said, thoughtfully, "I kind of like them!" he asserted in support.

"Daddy, she said it in front of a whole group of girls, and they all laughed at me."

"Sissy, I'm so sorry! I've told you kids many times that the saying 'sticks and stones will break my bones but words will never hurt me' is a saying that kids use to protect themselves from the emotional damage of harsh and unkind words.

"This adage is useful because it points out the ill will of the thoughtless assailant, and it gives strength back to the injured. The reason people use the "sticks and stones" saying is to protect themselves. The underlying truth is that nothing hurts more than cutting and hateful words. They break the heart in a way that no stone can.

"Your mom and I have tried very hard to teach both you and Sammy Junior to bite your tongue before you speak in anger or hate. That was so neither of you would ever say or do anything to hurt someone else. We all live in emotional glass houses to some extent. You must not let these thoughtless words hurt you too much. That little girl I'm sure has already forgotten. Just because someone says something doesn't make it true.

"You can learn something from the hurt. Learn to listen to the words that people use. Learn to decide for yourself if they are just talking in a hurtful way; and if they are, disregard what they say. Don't ever let thoughtless words steal your self-esteem or recklessly sway you about someone else." Dad looked at me, and I knew he felt everything I was feeling.

"I'll try, Daddy."

I began to think about the times Dad had told me that words could cut a person to the bone. At that moment all I could think about was the wish that my schoolmate had listened to a dad like mine.

SELF-ESTEEM: We all can be hurt by the words and actions of others. We can also be swayed by the destructive assertions of the brazen. Because someone asserts a position, it does not make it worthy or true. Each of us must personally evaluate a claim to determine its merit.

Tart Words make no Friends:
a spoonful of honey will catch more flies
than a Gallon of Vinegar.

–Poor Richard's Almanack, 1744

You Can Catch More Flies with Honey Than You Can with Vinegar

Animosity

"Shut that screen door, Suzanne Potter. You're letting all the flies in the house." Mom hollered at me from the kitchen.

As I slammed the backdoor screen closed, I hollered back, "I'm sorry, Mama."

Mom turned to Dad and said, "Will you get the flyswatter and kill these flies."

As I entered the kitchen, Dad was getting up to get the flyswatter, and he looked over at Mom and said, "Whatever happened to the old saying that you can catch more flies with honey than you can with vinegar? Did my expert skill with a flyswatter make that obsolete?"

Mom was not interested in horsing around and quickly responded with, "Just get rid of the flies, Sam. I don't care whether you use honey, vinegar, or a swatter. I just want them gone."

"You better duck, Suzanne. I am a man on a mission." Dad

giggled as he took out a couple of the flies that I had let in.

"Sissy, when you grow up, remember the old adage, 'You can catch more flies with honey than you can with vinegar.' It works with flies and it works with people. But if you want to please your mom, you best be darn good with a flyswatter and forget the honey and vinegar routine."

Sammy Junior and I watched, amazed, as Dad struck down fly after fly, some of them in midflight.

In later years, I started to reflect on the cleverness of this old proverb. I was surprised at the efficiency of its wisdom. In a very few words, it laid out the desired behavior, "catching flies." The old saying pointed out the wrong approach, vinegar, and then laid out a better plan, honey. Dad was trying to show Sammy Junior and me that some approaches to life were clearly better than others. This was concise behavior coaching. By asking the question "Am I using honey or vinegar?" we can evaluate our approach.

In Dad's simple way, he was teaching us statesmanship and leadership all in one sentence. Dad made it clear that to bully or intimidate was the hard path to productive human relationships. To improve our chances of any desired result, Dad taught us to align our actions with the needs of those we were trying to influence. All of that sophisticated teaching was done in the most unsophisticated way. Dad would just say, "You can catch more flies with honey than you can with vinegar."

I find it interesting that many corporate executives choose one path or the other. Corporate intimidators may experience temporary success, but intimidators rarely build support or long-term loyalty. Bullies create an underground of humanity, quiet in their anger as long as the intimidators wield control. This same underground will not give the extra mile; they will only give the minimum that they feel is required. The suppressed will wait and look for the moment when the intimidator loses power. Flies don't like vinegar and neither do human beings.

Statesmanship and leadership require the aligning of the goals of the team with the goals of the leader. It is the difference between freedom and oppression. True leadership builds mutual respect and a consensus to take a course of action. Bullies use emotional, physical, or financial intimidation. Good leaders use positive motivation as a tool. A poor leader uses negative motivation as a club. Honey or vinegar, which approach to life ultimately works?

ANIMOSITY: To influence others you either inspire or bludgeon. We can choose the positive or negative aspects of our character. We can bring forth a desired response best by using kindness, not animosity.

A lie will easily get you out of a scrape,
and yet, strangely and beautifully,
rapture possesses you when you have
taken the scrapes and left out the lie.

–C. E. Montague

Nobody Likes a Liar or a Cheat

Honesty

*I*t was bitter cold outside. The Christmas freeze had extended into January. It was fun to be out of school for the holiday; tomorrow I would have to return to first grade. Sammy Junior and I had a wonderful Christmas. Mom and Dad had been generous as usual, and we loved it. My new doll was beautiful, and I had gotten a large box of crayons. It was a sixty-four-count crayon box. There were so many colors and shades in that big box. There was even a white crayon!

Perplexed, I looked down at the box of colors. I couldn't figure out how to use the white crayon on the creamy-light manila art paper. Everything I tried just didn't show up.

As I struggled, frustration grew in my six-year-old brain. "What good is a white crayon if you can't see it!" I muttered to myself.

Finally, I had had it! A white crayon needed to be used on something dark! I got up with my white crayon in my tightly clenched fist. I was on a mission. As I rounded the corner from the living room and entered my mom's bedroom, I saw it. It was perfect—my answer.

Before I could think, my hand rapidly scribbled back and forth, back and forth. When I finally stopped, I realized that my white color marks were all over the side of Mom's dark mahogany chest. No sooner had I gratified the need to view my new crayon than reality began to creep upward racing from my hand to my brain. Suddenly, as if awakening from some overwhelming compulsion, I was afraid!

Ooh, was I going to get a real bad spanking for this one! Why didn't I think about what I was doing? But now it was too late, and was I going to get it!

About then, a ray of hope ignited in my brain.

I remembered Mom and Dad disliked lying more than just about anything. There was not much use in lying because the guilty party had to be either Sammy Junior or me. Mom always said, "You'll get in a whole lot less trouble in life if you just tell the truth in the first place."

Life has a few defining moments. This was mine. I decided to tell the truth and see if it really worked. Now, I wasn't brave enough to volunteer the truth. I kept hoping no one would notice the white marks up and down the side of the dark chest.

Yes, it was a childish delusion.

It wasn't long before I heard Mom shout, "Suzanne Potter, get yourself in here right now."

Shaking in fear, I approached as she asked me, "Who colored all over my dresser?"

"I did, Mommy, and I'm so sorry I did it," I muttered in a barely audible voice, totally afraid to raise my eyes off the floor.

What happened next was nothing short of a miracle. She bent down and hugged me and said, "Darling, I'm so proud of you for telling Mommy the truth! Your dad and I told you if you would learn to tell the truth you would not get in nearly as much trouble. I want you to know how important telling the truth is. I'm not going to punish you. I'll figure out a way to fix my chest. Just tell me you'll never do anything like this again."

I was so relieved I couldn't help but smile as I faithfully promised, "I promise, I promise, Mommy!"

As I left the bedroom, I knew I would never choose to lie again. I was convinced telling the truth was better. Once this decision was made, I never questioned its wisdom.

Dad had told me about George Washington, a story parents frequently told in the '40s. Children were encouraged to honor the truth by the popular story of George Washington and the cherry tree. My brain started to recall pieces of the story. George was young, just like me, when he cut down his dad's cherry tree. When George's dad confronted him, George did not compound the offense. He accepted his guilt and refused to lie. My dad never explained the story. He didn't have to. Dad, by telling me this story, was showing me the value he placed on honesty.

Truthfulness is such an integral part of integrity that, hundreds of years later, it is the central moment in the tale of George Washington and the cherry tree. This tale emphasizes the character of our first U.S. President.

The story about young George underscored the fact that human imperfections are real. Everyone makes bad choices; even the "father of our country" was not immune. Just like I knew that I should not have colored on Mom's chest, Washington knew he should not have cut down his father's cherry tree.

Cheating and lying are kissing cousins. Both vices are misrepresentations of the truth. Lying is the first step to cheating. Cheating is the first step to lying. It is easy to believe that no one will notice or count the times when we stretch the truth at work or cheat on our spouse. That philosophy misses the point. Character is about who we become. Character is our relationship with ourselves first, then others. We are approaching the point where "doing the right thing" is considered out of date. One thing is still true; we don't think it is out of date when it affects us directly. Even a cheater hates being cheated. A liar hates being lied to. When someone cheats you, you become outraged because the loss has an owner, and that owner is you. There is a universal law: give that which you wish to receive. It is an essential ingredient for a happy and satisfying life.

Good character is one of life's most valued assets. It is an asset that we can create, and no one else can take it from us. Sadly, a segment of our society has bought the lie that character doesn't really matter.

The principles that define what is right and what is wrong are fundamentals that stand constant over time. Our societal willingness to condone public breaches and excuse lying and infidelity because we do not see how it directly affects us misses the point.

Without character there can be no true self-esteem. Self-esteem must be earned to be real. It is earned in the quiet areas of life where only you know the truth. Peace of mind comes from aligning oneself with God's laws.

HONESTY: Be honest in all things. Honesty is so essential to defining character that it becomes unthinkable to value any achievement that lacks it. "Whoever can be trusted with very little can also be trusted with much, and whoever is dishonest with very little will also be dishonest with much." Luke 16:10

I always tell the truth.
I cannot be bothered to lie—
You need such a good memory.

–Sophia Loren

Don't Gild the Lily

Truth

*W*hen I was very young, I was quite prone to exaggerate. As a teenager, my verbal extremes would push Dad to rein me in with a somber, "Suzanne, don't you think you're gilding that lily." That was my cue to tone it down. As I matured, this adage disappeared from our dialogue.

Not long ago, I listened to a friend give an account of something I had previously witnessed. As he spoke, I was frustrated by his blatant misrepresentation. My friend thought the embellishment was more impressive. He told a client that something had been done when it had not. The embellishment made the client's situation sound as though more progress had been made in their behalf than had really occurred. My friend's willingness to enhance the truth was self-serving and potentially harmful to those who relied on the information. Suddenly, Dad's admonition, "Don't gild the lily," exploded in my brain with a clarity I had never experienced.

I never thought much one way or the other about this phrase.

I had seen no reason to wrestle with its meaning. Perhaps I led a sheltered life, or maybe I was just fortunate, but I had never observed this type of behavior pattern before. Candidly, I was troubled. I saw the embellishment as a trap, set and ready to snap shut. What would occur when the client's delivery date could not be met? Why had my friend lied when telling the truth was the ethical approach? With the truth, the client could begin to adjust their expectations. What if the time delay did not get made up along the way? I found myself awake in the middle of the night with this saying of my dad's returning to instruct me. I never understood the impact of its meaning when I was a child, and life had not given me any concrete examples—until now.

Weeks passed as I watched the pattern of minor deceptions repeat and expand. Sadness engulfed me. There was nothing wrong with the truth. The truth was not only acceptable but also defensible from the client's expectations. My friend felt compelled to expand the truth and make the situation sound far better than it was. For weeks the omissions and embellishments continued to weave a web, sticky and transparent, that finally snared the very spider that spun it.

Wisdom dictates that the simple, unadorned truth is sufficient. Truth has its own beauty and its own strength. It does not need our assistance. The proverb's warning is clear: gild the lily and risk losing your credibility—and the pure beauty of the "plain truth." Dad's wisdom, centuries old, still applies.

TRUTH: Character is not built or maintained with bold giant steps, but by resisting the small temptations. Truth is its own beauty. A distortion of the truth inevitably springs its own trap.

If you don't stand for something,
you will fall for anything.

–Ginger Rogers

I Done Jumped Up

Commitment

I wasn't eavesdropping, I just overheard. Mom and Dad were in the living room talking about a business commitment Dad had made.

"I said I would do it. Even though I really don't want to, I gave my word," I remember overhearing Dad tell Mom.

"Why don't you just call them, Dad, and tell them you've changed your mind?" I blurted out, as I stepped out of the hall into the living room with Mom and Dad. This quick suggestion was typical of my naïve and unsolicited advice. I was at that dangerous age, preteen, and I wanted to interact as an adult.

I wanted to know what the adults were doing. I wanted my opinion to be valued. So I invaded where a wiser Suzanne never would have gone. My need to be included in the adult decision-making altered my judgment relative to the respect my parents were due in private conversation.

Looking back over the decades since, I have to be amused at

my efforts. I can now appreciate my dad's tolerance for my rude intrusion. But I'll never forget his response. Dad stood there looking at me slightly surprised by the intrusion: "No, little girl, I can't change my mind. I done jumped up." Then he laughed.

Dad never explained. He didn't have to. I knew exactly what he meant.

In the society of the '50s, commitment and integrity were considered higher values than personal gratification. This value system became the backbone of the family and the framework that made business in the industrial society hum. Contract law was not the huge practice it is today. Business was done through verbal contracts based on the honor system. Dad's word was his bond. He would not think of overriding his personal integrity and his belief system just for the sake of convenience. "I done jumped up" meant that he had stepped forward and made a commitment, and commitments were to be honored.

In today's era of personal irresponsibility and lack of accountability, this saying invigorates like a breath of fresh air. It was a time when your word mattered. People could count on you to do what you promised, even if all the details were not contained in forty pages of legal specifics. There was value in maintaining the commitment. The commitment details were worked out later.

There is an undercurrent in Dad's statement: he wished he had not "jumped up." But, once up, breaking the commitment was out of the question.

COMMITMENT: More valuable than a smart man, a rich man, and a successful man is a man of integrity. Do what is right; say what you mean; mean what you say.

Let us be grateful to Adam, our benefactor.
He cut us out of the "blessing" of idleness
and won for us the "curse" of labor.

–Mark Twain

Bring Home the Bacon

Family Obligation

*I*t was Christmas sometime in the early '70s, and I was sitting in the den with Dad after a Christmas day turkey dinner. My two oldest girls were at play in the den with their Christmas bounty. Dad had just fixed a Mr. Potato Head face for little Suzy.

Dad turned to me, and in a rare somber moment said: "I'd never have left you kids or your mother no matter what life dealt us. A man ain't worth his salt if he won't provide for his family."

I only nodded in understanding. It was a rare comment from a man who hardly spoke about his emotions. At the time, I didn't think about the fact that Dad wasn't really talking about us. Dad was really talking about a father he never knew and a mother left to struggle alone with several small children. All I was ever told by Mom was that Dad's father left when he was a small child, and that his mother died of cancer when he was seventeen.

Dad was deeply committed to give something he had never

received; but, in truth, I am only guessing, since he never spoke of sadness or the past.

When I was very little, Dad would pack to leave for his week on the road. I would ask him "Daddy, where are you going?" It seems that I always got the same answer: "to bring home the bacon." Bringing home the bacon he saw as his job; it was what he did. I grew up with the idea that it was "the dad's" job to provide for the family. It was my dad's job to put food on the table as the "breadwinner." In the forties, the responsibility was clear and straightforward. Dad taught us to respect a good provider.

How a man chose to work and feed his family was to be respected regardless of the occupation, as long as it was "honest work." As Dad said, "there is no shame in honest work. The only shame is being too lazy to work."

Something we should all remember.

FAMILY OBLIGATION: When we bring children into this world, they are not only our joy but also our responsibility. The sex of the primary breadwinner may vary; but what time has not altered is the child's need to have parents with the character to act responsibly.

> *What is food to one man may be*
> *fierce poison to others.*
>
> –Lucretius

Clean Your Plate;
There Are Children Who Are Starving in China
Waste

*I*t was liver! Liver and onions! How can anything smell so delicious and taste so awful? Sammy Junior and I were brought up not to be wasteful, wasn't that enough? Did we have some civic duty to eat liver and onions?

Liver, we were told, is good for you. It is full of iron. The doctor told Mom that we should eat things like liver often to give our body all the iron it needed. After one taste, I was certain that I had all the iron I ever wanted. Mom and Dad could have testified, truthfully, that liver brought out my hardheaded streak and "iron" will.

I flat was not going to eat that stuff! To combat my stubbornness, Dad would offer Mom's favorite adage, "Clean your plate; there are children who are starving in China." The problem I had was finding a real connection to children a continent away.

It was impossible for me to comprehend that eating an awful dinner could help or hinder a child in China. China was too far away from our liver and onions to help anyone. Unfortunately, at the time, there was not a better adage that communicated the need to respect the cost and potential scarcity of food. My continued scorn for this saying covered dozens of tasty morsels—liver, beets, carrots, turnips, asparagus, and, above all else, pickled pig's feet! If I could not help China with liver, there is no way something as awful as beets could provide a benefit.

Mom and Dad were children of the Depression. I know that many times food was hard to come by and meager at best. Certainly my brother and I needed to be sensitive to waste and be grateful for what we had. But the mental reasoning of this frequently quoted adage was too far outside my rational and stubborn thinking. It was impossible to develop any motivation to make me oblige.

It was the "China" part that created the disconnect. China was a place I could not imagine. After all, I had never seen any children from China. TV was not around in the '40s to help my young mind understand the scope of our world. The wisdom just slipped by.

Children of my generation would have understood more if we had simply been told that many children went to bed hungry, and it was disrespectful of their need to take more food out on our plate than we felt we could eat. I suppose this adage was ultimately useful because, over time, I came to understand the underlying message. I wasn't uncaring child, but liver, and possibly beets, posed an insurmountable obstacle.

WASTE: Wasteful behavior is disrespectful to the less fortunate. Wastefulness actively throws away the item it took effort to provide. People of integrity do not dishonor the work effort or needs of others.

Doctors bury their mistakes;

lawyers hang them.

But journalists put theirs

on the front page.

–Anonymous

You Made Your Bed, Now Lie in It

Responsibility

"Suzanne Pitty-Pot, your mother told you yesterday to wash and dry the dishes, and they are still sitting there," Dad was reminding me again.

"Daddy, don't make me do them. They are all yucky. Mom always fills up the sink with soapy water, but it's all cold and slimy now. Please, pretty please, won't you just get the water out of the sink for me?"

I really hated sticking my hand into the cold, dirty water to release the drain. I had to start over by filling the sink with hot, soapy water. Even rubber gloves wouldn't help because the cold water was too deep. If I put the gloves on, the water would fill up the gloves spilling over into the gloves from the top as I tried to pull out the stopper.

"Suzanne, didn't I hear your mom tell you last night that she had filled the sink with hot, soapy water and for you to come and do the dishes?" Dad reminded me, and I knew what was coming next.

Dad was not to be swayed. "Suzanne, you made your bed, now lie in it!"

I was getting a dose of my father's strong medicine. When he dusted off this one, I knew stuff had hit the fan. You can bet your Texas boots that I wasn't Dad's sweetie pie then. I was definitely in the doghouse. When I did something really bad like sass Mom or pick a fight with my brother, I was punished. If I complained or tried to talk my way out of punishment, Dad was firm.

I knew the rules of behavior. The Potter household did not have many rules, but the rules were not open to discussion. I was taught to be accountable to the rules at home and in life. Mom and Dad had fair and reasonable expectations. They did not have so many rules that it was hard to remember them all. But I did test them on occasion.

I was taught accountability and personal responsibility consistently as a child, and I firmly believe I became a better adult because of it.

Sometimes, I see behavior that seeks to shift personal responsibility to a more convenient target. This behavior makes me want to say: "If you made your bed, why do you expect the rest of us to have to lie in it?"

RESPONSIBILITY: Our actions create our results, and we need to take responsibility for our own actions. We cannot develop character until we are willing to assume personal responsibility for our lives.

What Goes Around, Comes Around

Justice and Revenge

I grew up in a time when neighbors were people you knew. The world was a smaller place running on a slower clock. The world I was born in was a privileged world. I was an American child. We had a home with an indoor bath. We had an icebox with a weekly delivery of ice to keep our food fresh. We could leave the windows and doors unlocked because the world around us was safe. The milkman delivered the milk and set it inside the front door. If people came through our neighborhood homeless and hungry, we were not taught to fear them. We offered food to those who were "down on their luck."

As a child, I had no way to recognize or understand the privilege of being born an American. It takes time and life experiences to build that appreciation.

In the '40s, the impact of the automobile was just starting to affect American family life. Many families did not own cars. I did not know a family with two cars. The radio shows were our entertainment and our only source of exposure outside our microcosm, the neighborhood. Television was just beginning on snow-filled black and white screens. It engaged both eyes and ears in the awareness of our world. Television was yet to be a major entertainment medium; it was too young—a novelty. The growth of television and the growth of the automobile changed our world in fundamental ways.

As society grew larger and more mobile, evil had more access. Evil had visibility. Evil had the mobility to distance itself from its evil acts and hide among the enlarged numbers of our society. As evil in our society became more pronounced, it gave rise to vulnerability and self-awareness everywhere.

Air-conditioning, the final disconnect, gave people final permission to lock themselves up inside their home. The home had to become more secure as protection from the unknown evil outside. The wisdom of Will Rogers, famous for his saying, "I never met a man I didn't like," was replaced with "Never talk to strangers."

As life evolved from the safe gentleness of my childhood to the frighteningly dangerous world of today, my dad tried to explain, "what goes around, comes around." Dad believed that the action you take comes back to you, multiplied many times over. Goodness was its own reward; bad behavior would catch up with you in time. "What goes around comes around," so obvious to Dad, took years for me to understand and trust.

In many ways, this saying also builds on the foundation laid by the Golden Rule. Dad understood that we can control only ourselves, no one else. If we would all adopt the Golden Rule, the other problems of man's relationship to man would disappear. Dad made it clear that it was not our job to become the self-appointed judge of others. It was reassuring to know that the guilty will be punished. "What goes around comes around" assured justice when bullies took advantage and seemed to be no worse off. This belief made justice available when the sharp, false tongues of gossip spread hurtful ideas. It promised justice to victims of horrible crimes that seemed to go unpunished. When justice appears to have failed on earth; eternity looms ahead.

JUSTICE AND REVENGE: "What goes around, comes around" verbalizes "we get what we give" in another way. Evil returns to the perpetrator in one form or another somewhere down the road. Ultimately, "What we sow, we will reap." The seeds of bad character grow their own bitter fruit.

Tell me thy company, and I'll
tell thee what thou art.

–Miguel de Cervantes

Birds of a Feather Flock Together

Influence of Friends

*I*t was late on a Saturday evening, and my girl-friend and I were standing outside the Texas Theater waiting for Dad to pick us up after the show. As we stood outside waiting, we noticed a group of boys from the junior high hanging around. Laughing loudly, these teens were making fun of a group of much younger boys. The belligerent group seemed to feel quite smug and impressed with themselves as they all lit up their Camel cigarettes. Their sole mission in life was to look tough and act in charge. They wanted to look big, and they believed the key to that image was to smoke. Even as a seventh-grader, I could see through the act and the attempts to look grown up. I was not impressed.

As Dad drove up, I noticed a frown come across his face as he saw the group of boys. I knew that Dad hated smoking. As we got into the car, all he said was, "birds of a feather flock together."

My mind raced back through the years to all Dad's warnings about choosing friends. Dad had said that the friends you choose are critical. To stay friends you must have things in common. If your friends do well in school, you will want to do well in school. If your friends struggle in school, you will not want to make them feel worse by pushing to achieve more. You will either lose a friend or begin to undervalue your own education. Dad cautioned me that as I grew up I would have to guard the direction of my own life. The direction of my life could be seen in the "birds" I flew with.

Dad's advice was to evaluate the "flock" I was in and determine if I wanted to go where they were headed. If the answer was no, then even as a teenager, I must have the fortitude and intelligence to find a better "flock."

INFLUENCE OF FRIENDS: Choose your friends carefully and observe the traits in those you befriend. Ask yourself if those are the traits that you want to adopt.

It's not how old you are
but how you are old.

–Marie Dressler

Too Soon Oldt, Too Late Smarts

Wisdom

*D*ad would grin and his soft blue eyes would sparkle as he uttered, "too soon oldt, too late smarts." It was as though Dad had a secret that was shared by him and some unknown German kindred spirit. I am not certain, but I always suspected that this adage came from an old cartoon. It is too far in the past to find out now, but Dad loved it! I think he held onto this phrase because he shared the view that youth is wasted on the young. Dad's view included his own youth. He understood that he, in his own youth, had left so much untapped potential. That untapped potential was visibly seen through the perspective of life experience. The young are foolish and not yet seasoned enough to appreciate what they have. This adage contemplates the process of attaining wisdom.

When I was young, we were still deep in the industrial age. Today, we live in an information age and a knowledgeable society. Knowledge, information, and education have become the currency of our times. Rarely do we hear a conversation that discusses wisdom.

Wisdom is distilled from firsthand experience and inward reflection on that experience. Those who seek it only acquire wisdom over time. Wisdom is a word we seem to have forgotten. Its use has fallen out of favor. If we do not hear the word, could it be that it is something we no longer value? Today, we seek intellectual capital as a meager substitute. With all the emphasis on knowledge and information, we have missed the broader need—a need for wisdom.

Dad's expression was not referring to book smarts. He was addressing the "smarts" that come over time with life reflection. He was talking about acquiring wisdom. "Too soon oldt, too late smarts" was his way of wistfully glancing backward. The phrase implied a wish that wisdom could be achieved at an earlier age. It was light-hearted with a sad undercurrent. The unspoken longing was for the wisdom to live life better, more intelligently, and more fully.

Decades have passed and even though Dad forewarned me, I still found myself, as predicted, "too soon oldt, too late smarts."

WISDOM: Time leads to experience. Experience leads to knowledge. Knowledge by itself does not lead to wisdom. Knowledge with reflection can lead to understanding. Wisdom is found by mixing large doses of reflection with a generous helping of self-evaluation. Wisdom is not born; it is created within. A person can have character without much wisdom, but one cannot attain wisdom without character and reflection.

Man is always more than he
can know of himself;
consequently his accomplishments,
time and time again,
will come as a surprise to him.

–Golo Mann

Whatever You Do,
Be the Best You Can Be

Achievement

"**D**addy, am I dumb?" I was asking, but almost afraid to hear his answer.

"Of course not, Sissy! Why would you think such a thing?" Clearly Dad was surprised by my question.

"Well, the teacher at kindergarten sat me at the long, low table with five other kids, and everybody else was seated at big desks. I think we were put at the low table because the teacher doesn't think we are as smart as everybody else."

"Well I don't believe any of the other children are any smarter than the six of you sitting at that table. There is probably another explanation. Maybe the room just ran out of desks. Besides, Sweetheart, all Mom and I expect from you is for you to just try to be the best you can be. That is all any of us can do. As long as you work at becoming the best you can be, then you'll do just fine." Dad smiled and gave my hand a soft squeeze.

"You know, you are pretty smart, Suzie Q, because you can beat me at checkers. You have to be pretty sharp to beat your old man at checkers. Now quit worrying; you are just in kindergarten. It will be years before you or the teachers know where your talents lie. Just relax and have fun."

Dad and Mom never told us that they expected us to make "A" grades in school. They never told us they expected "Bs" either. They just asked that we always do our best. Sometimes, I think that is harder, because how do you really know what your best is? There is no timeline on becoming your best. It is a moving target. Becoming one's best sets a very tough standard but one, that by definition, is attainable.

Because the expectation was fair, it was one that drove me to constant improvement. Because I sensed love and tolerance in the standards that Mom and Dad set, I felt the desire to show them my love by focusing my effort on becoming better. Becoming the best I could be had a clear application to my life as a student and my life as an employee. Dad asked us to apply this standard across the board to all aspects of life.

ACHIEVEMENT: Why live a life that does not let us know what we could have been or could have created? The only way to answer the question is to apply life's lesson of becoming the best you can be.

If you have built castles in the air,

your work need not be lost;

that is where they should be.

Now put foundations under them.

–Henry David Thoreau

Rome Wasn't Built in a Day

Patience

$\mathcal{A}$s I stood looking at the gray, muddy mush that Earl Dee was pouring into big square frames, I turned to Dad and asked, "When can I swing, Daddy?"

He looked surprised that I would ask such a question. The surprised expression faded only to be replaced by his familiar wide grin "Keely-locks (Dad's name for me when I was very young), you've got to be patient just a little longer. I'll tell you what. As soon as the concrete hardens just a little bit more, we'll put your initials in it, okay?"

"Uh-huh," I nodded my head.

Earl Dee, Dad's brother, was building the most incredible swing set in our backyard. He had been working on it for weeks on a part-time basis. It was exciting for Sammy Junior and me to watch the work as it progressed, but it had taken so long that I was getting anxious. I wanted to play.

"I want to swing, Daddy! When will the cement be dry?" I nagged.

"Sissy, hold your horses! Rome wasn't built in a day!"

I had no idea where or what Rome was. I was too young for Dad's reference to make sense, but I did know what Dad meant when he said I should "hold my horses," so I figured that his comment on Rome must mean something similar.

Often, I heard Dad say both things when he wanted me to wait. In the ensuing years, Dad would use the adage "Rome wasn't built in a day" to encourage Sammy Junior and me to be diligent in our pursuit of learning. Dad cautioned us to respect the reality of how progress occurs. Personal progress is like building a building. Much of the time spent in building something takes place before the building actually takes visual shape. The complete building does not appear until much later, after a lot of the invisible work has taken place.

Some situations in life can appear futile when, in reality, much that is vitally important has occurred. Foundations for important structures take more time before results are seen than foundations for smaller and less important buildings.

"Rome wasn't built in a day" is another way of saying "patience is a virtue." Accomplishment is built one stone on top of another. The visual metaphor of life being built stone upon stone over many years was more graphic than some of the other proverbs. It gave perspective on learning and skill development. Later, when I would start elementary school, Dad had already set the stage for me to understand the slow process that education would represent.

Each area of life opens an opportunity to build something of value inside us. The life we build becomes as real as any architectural creation. The vast empire that Rome created was a metaphor that helped Sammy Junior and me comprehend and deal with the frustrations of the educational process.

Life can be a tribute to the time we are on earth, or it can be spent just marching in time, going nowhere, learn nothing, doing little. The greatest gift we can leave behind is strong, kind, caring children who will grow up as an asset to society at large. The greatest gift we as children can give back to our parents is to become the kind of human being that makes them proud. Character development, integrity, knowledge, and wisdom are works in progress.

PATIENCE: It takes time plus patience to build a better you.

So they often spend their most precious asset,
their time, and wander through life
without much of a plan.

–Robert Kiyosaki

Time Waits For No Man

Gift of Life

*L*ooking at me over his newspaper, Dad said, "Well, tell me, Suzie, can that dude dance or not?"

It was Sunday morning, and the night before I had gone to a teen formal dance at Kiest Park Clubhouse. We had a live disc jockey, and we all did "The Bop" and danced to popular rock and roll songs by Little Richard and Elvis Presley.

"He was pretty good, Dad. But I got to dance with quite a few others, so it was fun."

"Well, I'm glad you had fun. You'll be grown up and gone before you know it. It is a shame, but time waits for no man, and you'll find that it won't wait for any little girls, either."

For some reason, Dad's words made me feel melancholy. I suppose I sensed a feeling of loss. I sensed the loss of opportunities and things not done.

I know that Dad meant to state a simple fact of life. Dad was telling me to take advantage of life before it passed by. He always encouraged me to pack my life with fun, work, and learning. Time and life are finite and precious. Indecision and inaction wastes life. The things we do in life, even those things that do not work out, do not create the sense of loss in our life. The regrets of life are for the things we never tried.

We sense our loss of opportunity and begin to feel regret when our time on earth is in its later stages. Things we failed to do haunt us. It is not so much the failure to accomplish that haunts, as it is the failure to try. It becomes the not knowing that is sad. We do not know whether we could have created a better life if we had done more, and we all know we could have done more.

I am thankful for this saying. It has caused me to reflect on a life that hid in the shadows of what it could have been. I knew early on that I did not want that kind of life. Today, I fight the fears that hold back my decision to live life fully.

When Dad teased, "Time marches on," I knew that life could be an exciting parade that I could join. I connected the two thoughts together and decided that I did not want to stand in place, marking time. I wanted to be part of the parade. I wanted to take action and march.

GIFT OF LIFE: Take full advantage of every opportunity that life offers, or the time to take advantage of that opportunity may pass you by.

I couldn't wait for success,
so I went ahead without it.

–Jonathan Winters

Where There Is a Will, There Is a Way

Determination

Willpower was Dad's secret ingredient. No IQ test can define it, and no teacher can quantify it. For Dad, willpower was the ultimate competitive edge. When I complained to Dad about how hard school was or how mistreated I felt, he would quickly interrupt with simple advice, "where there is a will there is a way." He believed that understanding the power of determination early in life made all the difference in the journey we took and the life results we created.

Dad's wisdom came from experience. He knew that everything started and stopped in the mind. Our mind is the unique gift that God gave us at birth. Our challenge is to use this gift in the ways God intended. All asset creation starts with two critical ingredients: a goal and a will. A strong will is the fuel that drives us toward the goal. It is the will to continue that gives dreams the opportunity to survive and grow.

I would go to Dad seeking sympathy for homework that I was trying to avoid or sidestep, but he gave me no room to quit. Dad's "where there is a will, there is a way" attitude increased my frustration, but it forced me back to the problem for continued effort. As mad as I got with his lack of sympathy, I knew he was right. I kept my frustration to myself and went back to the struggle at hand. I remember grumbling, "If there was a way to do the homework, why didn't Dad just cut through the nonsense and show me the way?"

I'll never know the answer to that question, because I never had the nerve to ask such a blunt and disrespectful question. I know that Dad's measured response forced me to find my own way and develop my own will. Ultimately, Dad's lesson taught me more than the school assignment I found so frustrating.

The greatest prize in the world for me was praise from Dad. His praise was lavish, warm, abundant, and above all, genuine. Both Mom and Dad watered the garden of our self-esteem. To do well, I believe that every child must grow a well-cultivated garden of self-esteem. Dad praised effort as much as accomplishment.

Mom and Dad bragged to their friends about how smart my brother and I were. They worked as a team to make us feel special; Sammy Junior and I knew they were proud of us. I don't think that Sammy Junior and I were particularly exceptional, but the warm light of praise from my father and mother gave both my brother and me the will to improve our grades in school.

Dad knew how to motivate. Praise was his positive reinforcement tool. It was up to us to find the way to earn the praise. In elementary school, my report cards were barely average. Elementary school was hard for me. Dad always wanted to review our report cards. Somehow, he gleaned an area to praise, even when very few positive things existed. One report card was so weak that the only praise he could find was a plus mark in class conduct. As unimpressive as my early report cards were, I never developed any negative feelings about report cards because Dad found a way to praise and encourage me for a better performance next time. I did not work for the grades or what the knowledge would later do for me; I worked for the praise. I was too young to understand the value of mind development, but my father knew, and he tended the garden of my mind with the love of an expert gardener.

Back in the '40s and '50s, we were told that IQ was something you were born with and could do nothing about. Personally, I don't believe this long-held theory. I believe that drive and work can increase an individual's intelligence. I believe it because I did just that, through sheer force of will. My grades improved slowly, one year after the next, every year throughout my education. I could sense my brain building on the hard-earned tools and the skills of the year before.

It was my inner secret. I was not smart. I was just more driven. That drive became my quiet, secret weapon for life. I was always willing to work harder and longer than others, and that "will" is what paid off. It was not the aptitude or the IQ.

I developed a deep appreciation for the relationship between will and all forms of outstanding accomplishment. The saying "where there is a will, there is a way" says enough. No one needs to show you the way. If you have the will, you will find the way.

Willpower is more important than skill. It is critical to life achievement. There is no inherent time limit on this historic saying, no promise of a quick fix or prompt result. Just the simple formula:

WILL = WAY

DETERMINATION: Determination is the force that moves us forward. It moves us over, under, around, and through the obstacles in life.

No book is of much importance;
the vital thing is
what do you yourself think?
–Elbert Hubbard

Use Your Head; You're Not Thinking

Intellect

I was sitting in front of the TV with my algebra homework in my lap. Dad was watching *I Love Lucy* with me as I worked. I was struggling with a difficult word problem. It was a real mind bender. I read the whole problem repeatedly, but it was too long and confusing for my mind to wrestle it into submission. Since Dad was handy, I said, "Daddy, I can't figure out this math problem, can you help me?"

"Suzie, it has been too long for me to remember much algebra. Besides, it doesn't seem to me like you've been working at it for very long. Use your head, Suzanne, you are not thinking."

Dad was right. I gave up quickly because I knew he was there. Thinking is the hardest work there is, and I wanted him to do the hard stuff. I had read the problem, but I really did not want to put the full mental energy into the effort of solving it. Tough algebra problems require a systematic and step-by-step analytical approach. It was hard mental work. Dad's advice, "Use your head; you're not thinking," identified the obstacle to my algebra problem. I was mentally lazy. I had spent little effort trying to solve it for myself. I wanted the easy way out. I wanted someone else to do my thinking.

Amusingly enough, my dad believed early on that I had the capacity for logical thought. I wonder if I would have ever found the road to using my head had Dad been less certain that I could do it. As I have aged, I have grown to appreciate the difference between information and thinking.

In our society, it is possible to do well in the educational process without doing much in the way of thinking. A very high percentage of learning is memory learning—seeing and hearing information and retaining it for future use. Spelling is like that. Spelling and arithmetic are essentially memory learning. Algebra and essay composition were the first disciplines to introduce linear thinking as a fundamental part of the educational process.

"Use your head," from Dad's perspective, meant to think and use "good old horse sense." Dad admired common sense because it relies on logic. As far as Dad was concerned, book learning was useless without common sense to go along with it.

Thoughts are our creative resource. Memorized knowledge can provide tools, which advance this creative skill. Mostly in life, we are engaged in repetitive acts. Very little time is left for creative endeavors. Great discoveries have come from asking empowering questions and seeking their answers.

Questions such as: If we could go to the moon, how would we do it? Once Kennedy set the goal of landing on the moon, the scientific community scrambled. "How in the world would we do it?" With the right question, you ultimately get the right answer.

Our president forced the scientific community to rise to the challenge. It was more than a call to action; it was a call for results.

Kennedy's call was a historic example of, "Use your head; you're not thinking." Just imagine where our focused minds can take us.

INTELLECT: Thinking determines action. Action determines results. Spend time in thought and develop your thinking processes.

It's a funny thing about life;
if you refuse to accept anything but the best,
you very often get it.

–W. Somerset Maugham

Life Won't Give You What You Want;
It Will Give You What You Will Accept

Life Strategy

$\mathcal{T}$he difference between going with the flow and charting a course is vast. Clearly, it is easier to go with the flow, and that is what most of us do most of the time. Dad used to say that "life won't give you what you want; it will give you what you will accept." I wish I had heard this from him more often or at least paid more attention to its meaning. Sometimes, life can seem such a struggle that any solution is welcomed, as long as it comes quickly and changes the burden we are facing. For example, when we get out of school and need a job, any job seems better than none. But where we start creating our income can have long-lasting effects. Understanding what we want, not what others want, and seizing control of our lives is crucial.

This idea first confronted me as a new high school graduate. Before starting college, I found a summer job at Union Bankers Life Insurance in downtown Dallas. I worked in the posting department for incoming health insurance premiums. In those days, all posting was done manually. It took less than a week to master the complexities of the job. Needless to say, it was boring, repetitive, and not challenging. I had only been at the job two weeks when one night at dinner Dad asked me how I liked my new job. "Well, actually, I hate it!" I said with complete conviction. "I just hope I can stand it three months till college starts."

I think Dad was surprised by my intensity. What I didn't tell him was that the other young girls and older women I was working with were shocking to me. They clearly had different values and morals from the ones I had been raised with. The supervisor's attitude toward the customer was less than ethical, and I was dismayed at her attitude. The ethical differences were so pronounced that I could hardly wait for five o'clock to roll around. I was courteous, but at work I said little and I observed a great deal. It was during that summer job that I developed a deep appreciation for the privilege of going to college. I knew that college would give me the opportunity to be more selective where I worked and with whom I worked. I knew with utter clarity what I did not want. I did not ever want to be trapped in a job working with people I didn't like or respect. Education represented more choices, and I wanted those choices.

Who really controls our life? Are we looking for what others offer or are we looking for what we want? To get what we want, we must know what we want and go get it ourselves.

It took me too many years to realize that I had the responsibility to go and seek what I wanted. My dreams were not going to come to me. Taking the initiative in our lives is a basic tenet of scripture: "seek and ye will find." Scripture does not say sit still and opportunity will find you. If we do not get clarity on what we want, we do not know what we want to seek. If we do not know what to seek, we will be forced to wait, hope, and take the crumbs life tosses us.

LIFE STRATEGY: Measure all major decisions against the possibility that you could and should demand more for yourself. Decide what it is you truly want for yourself, and don't compromise.

.

We must leave exactly on time . . .
From now on everything
must function to perfection.
—Benito Mussolini

Might Doesn't Make Right

Power

"*I* don't understand, Miss Stedman. Are you telling me that you don't think I can pass algebra?" I was in the midst of the most important decision in my school life. The choice I made would affect my entire education. Miss Stedman was my eighth grade arithmetic teacher, and eighth grade was where the men were separated from the boys, so to speak. Ninth grade would draw the line between the strong math students and the weak ones.

I knew I wasn't the most talented kid in arithmetic, but I felt that I understood it. Memorization and speed were not my strengths. But then again, in the eighth grade nothing much appeared to be my strength. This was not the time to go with the flow. It was decision time. I fully understood how important this choice was going to be.

Each eighth grader was given a counseling period with his or her math teacher. It was the teacher's duty to sort through the students and push them toward the correct math course for the following year.

Miss Stedman told me that in her "humble opinion," I was not capable of passing algebra and that it would be "wise" to put it off and take general math instead. I was frightened and embarrassed. I knew Dad was counting on me going to college. If I didn't take algebra, I wasn't sure I could get into a good university. So I asked Miss Stedman just one question: "Miss Stedman, if I want to go to college, how many years of advanced math do I have to have in order to be admitted?"

"Well, all colleges require at least three years and some are requiring four years," she responded.

Inside, I was upset. She had not even brought up my desire to go to college. What if I hadn't asked the question and took her advice and then found out that I didn't have the right courses to be admitted into college. I would break Dad's heart!

"Well, I don't know, Miss Stedman. I don't think I have any choice if I want to get into college. I have to take four years of advanced math, and it seems like the only choice I have is to take algebra now."

"Suzanne, I really hate to see you do it. I don't think you are ready for it, and I don't think you can handle it. Most students have a real hard time with algebra. We don't have to turn in your choice until tomorrow. Tell your parents what I said, and let me know tomorrow."

I went home frightened. I felt the burden of this decision. It was midweek and Dad was on the road. I decided that I wouldn't tell Mom. This was a decision I would have to make on my own. If I wasn't working in high school to go to college, what was I doing? If I didn't go to college, what would I do? Algebra seemed like the only door to go into. General math opened the door to a path I had no desire to travel.

The next day, as I sat terrified in Miss Stedman's class, I was afraid that she would try to dominate and alter my decision. I had never challenged the wisdom of an adult authority figure before. I knew Miss

Stedman's intentions were good. I had always been taught to respect my elders, and Miss Stedman was about as "elder" as they came. She looked too old to be alive, much less teach. Just because it was her opinion that I should take general math didn't make it right for me.

I was going to take algebra, period! It was the only path to my goal of college, and that was that. I was using self-talk to tighten my resolve. As expected, Miss Stedman tried again to push me into the general math class, but I held to my decision. This was the first major life decision I had ever made. And it turned out to be one of the best decisions I ever made.

I reported to Mrs. Priest's algebra class the following year, and I loved both Mrs. Priest and algebra. I embraced algebra and it embraced me back. It became my all-time favorite course, and it was a breeze. I found that I loved the analytical process. Miss Stedman was dead wrong. Memorizing multiplication tables and doing them under time pressures were not my strengths, but the analytical thinking that dominated algebra was my cup of tea. Finally, I was good at something in school!

I've often wondered what might have happened if I had buckled under the heavy intimidation of a powerful adult. Dad had warned me many times that "might doesn't make right." But I always thought he was only talking about physical might. I had never explored the might of intimidation. If might does not make something right, what does?

I have come to my own conclusions, as each of us must. For me, it means that most popular opinions could also be wrong. Certainly that is the implication of this saying. If consensus and might do not make something right, then the inevitable conclusion is that we must find and follow "right" on our own.

POWER: Political power, popular opinion, and physical strength can be imposed on others, but their force never makes them right. To find out what is right, whether it be a personal decision or a political position, we must engage our minds, sort the information, and act upon our conclusions whether "might" is for us or against us. "Most men would rather die than think. Many do." Bertrand Russell

We can have more than we've got
because we can become more than we are.

—Jim Rohn

Your Reach Should Exceed Your Grasp

Learning

𝑰t was late afternoon, and June Trammell was get-
ting in her mom's car to head home. June was my high school debate
partner and best friend. As she started to leave, I hollered, "If you get
there first, save me a seat. If I get there first, I'll save you a seat. But
hurry! I can only hold the seat so long!"

June and I were working out our schedules for the new school
year. When school opened, we could take our approved courses,
arrange our schedule, and "run for our teachers." The first students
to the room filled the course and closed the class. If you didn't make
your first choice, you quickly left and ran for the second choice.

Running for classes required a strategic plan. The goal was to
get all your first choice teachers by reaching the room before it filled
up. The longer the distance between each run, the more your likelihood of beating other students diminished. Running from one side of
the school to the other and moving between stories in a three-story
building could create a considerable challenge. If the run was too far

and the teacher was extremely popular, you didn't have a prayer of getting your first choice.

As June drove off, Dad came out to retrieve the evening paper. As he leaned over to pick up the paper, he said; "What are you girls plotting now? I never saw so many pieces of paper on the living room floor."

"Daddy, we have to run for classes tomorrow, and Sunset High is three stories. The teachers I want are always on the opposite sides of the building from one another. June and I were planning the seventh period so that we could be together. To do that we have to manipulate our schedule so that we don't have too far to run between any single period. If we get shut out of any single class earlier in the periods, it could throw the whole strategy off."

"Well, what happens if you don't get the teachers you want?" Dad's interest was piqued.

"Well, I'd have to go for second, third, or last choice, but that is part of the strategy."

"What do you mean by that, Sissy?" Dad seemed intrigued.

"Well, by the time you waste the run time on your first choice and then lose out, the other kids who want a safe bet have already filled the second or third choices. The kids who risk going for their first choice could easily be part of the no-fill and end up with the last choice teachers. Some reward for trying to get the best." As I spoke, I could see Dad was beginning to understand the need for all the paper. Each sheet was a different strategy. Plan A, first choice, and plans B and C, if plan A failed.

"Aren't most of the teachers pretty good?" he asked.

"Yes, but some are better than others," I responded.

"You'll be okay," he tried to reassure.

Suddenly, I began to dump my fears. "Well, Daddy, I am really afraid of the run for junior English. Most of the teachers are really hard and strict. I can only schedule English in sixth period because of my other electives. The two best choices for sixth period English are as far as possible from my Spanish class at fifth period. English is the one that really has me worried. It is my worst subject, and I wanted Miss Ferguson. She's supposed to be funny and not too hard. I need an easy teacher!"

"I'm scared to death that I'll get stuck with Hattie Lee Hornbeck. Miss Hornbeck is supposed to be the hardest English teacher in the school. Her students always have more homework, and everyone says she is tough!"

"Can I ask you a question about Miss Hornbeck?" Dad responded quietly.

"Sure, Daddy. What?"

"Do you think the kids who got stuck with Miss Hornbeck feel like they learned anything?"

"Yes, sir," I responded, sensing where he was headed. "A lot of the kids who are real smart in English say they learned more in her class than they had in the last three years. But a "C" in her class is like an "A" or "B" in the other teachers' classes."

Dad's face softened, and his blue eyes studied mine. He began to tell me what he really thought.

"Well," he started slowly. "It seems to me you win no matter what happens. If you get the teachers you want, you learn a little English, and you have a pretty good chance of looking good on paper for college with an "A." If you are forced to take English under Miss Hornbeck, even if you don't get the grades, you are going to learn more in her class, and it is bound to pay off later by making college easier. If it were up to me, I'd tell you that I bet Miss Hornbeck isn't as hard as your mind figures she is, and I bet you'd do a lot more growing there. But you have to pace yourself as to what you can handle."

He took a long pause. "Just remember, Sissy, this is more about *you* getting better than it is about getting better grades. Never underestimate what you can do, because you really don't know what that is yet. Just make sure that *your reach always exceeds your grasp,* or you're just not growing! I love you, little girl; it will all work out! Don't worry either way. Trust your judgment, and just do it."

LEARNING: To grow is uncomfortable. Growth by definition takes place outside our comfort zones. Only by growing intellectually do we become more capable, competent, independent, and self-assured. Face the fear and change the future.

People are getting smarter nowadays;
they are letting lawyers,
instead of their conscience, be their guide.

–Will Rogers

Let Your Conscience Be Your Guide

Source of Character

*L*ewis had just called and asked me, a junior, to go with him to the senior prom. I told him I needed to let Mom use the phone, but that I would call him back in a few minutes. I was in a state of panic. I didn't know what to do. Lewis was a great friend but never a boyfriend. He was not asking me as a girlfriend to go to the dance. He just didn't want to miss the special event, and the girl of his heart, Anne, would not give him the time of day. Lewis just wanted to have fun and not miss his senior prom.

It was exciting to think about going to the prom at the Statler Hilton. All the girls would get to wear beautiful prom dresses, and there was the elegant dinner before the dance. What girl would not want to go? Maybe me. Maybe I should not accept, even though I was dying to go.

My reason for hesitation was June, my best friend. June and I were active in the debate club, and we were the number-one girls team at Sunset. We went on debate trips all over Texas and

Oklahoma. It was great fun, and the fellowship between all the debaters was great. Lewis and James were one of the top-ranked boys teams and one of the best in the state. The debaters all hung out together and were simply best of friends.

Unfortunately, June was secretly crazy about Lewis. To Lewis, June and I were just pals, part of a large circle of debate friends. Lewis would never get over his love for Anne. I wanted to go to the dance and have fun, but I didn't want to hurt June. What was I going to do?

I knew instantly. Dad was home. I'd go ask him what to do!

I went through all the long-winded emotional explanation, and he sat quietly until I was through. Then he asked me, "Well, what do you want to do, little girl?"

"I don't know!" I blubbered in panic. "That's why I asked you!"

"I can't make that decision for you, Sissy. You are old enough to make your own decisions," he said with a firmness that I did not want to hear. "Do you know what you want to do?" he asked.

"Well, yes and no," I responded. "I've always wanted to go to the prom. Every junior girl hopes she will get asked. But I love June, and I don't want to hurt her. I just don't know what to do, Daddy. Can't you help me?"

"Sissy, this is one you need to do yourself. You'll live with the decision you make, and you had better be the one to think it through. Go in the other room all by yourself, calm down, and get real still. Then listen carefully to your conscience. Let that be your guide. You're a good person. Your conscience will lead to the answer you need. Just have faith in what you feel, and then go do what is right."

An hour later I came back into the den. I was relieved and happy. I had my answer and all was well. I had decided to call June and find out what she wanted me to do. Eventually, she would find out anyway, no matter which decision I made. Dad was right—my conscience knew exactly what to do. Dad knew that to develop character I had to learn to make tough decisions, and I needed to take the personal responsibility for my own character. Dilemmas can be difficult, but your conscience, if you listen, can find true north and lead you in the right direction.

SOURCE OF CHARACTER: There is a moral center in each of us if we "learn and discern" how to hear it and how to follow it. The Holy Spirit guides and comforts us through our conscience. God gave you Him for a reason. ". . . I am not lying, my conscience confirms it in the Holy Spirit." Romans 9:1

Ther nis no werkman, whatsoevere he be,
That may bothe werke wel and hastily.

–Geoffrey Chaucer

There Are Only Twenty-Four Hours in a Day

Priorities

"Suzanne, S U Z A N N E! You better get up! It is already nearly one o'clock in the afternoon!" I could faintly hear Mom yelling.

"Oh, no! Not really! Tell me I didn't sleep that late!" I awoke with a start.

It was Saturday. I had a major exam on Monday morning in Western Civilization, and I needed every study hour possible to get ready. I thought I had set the alarm for 7:00 A.M. I must have shut it off in my fatigue and gone back to sleep.

SMU, where I went to school, was on the other side of Dallas from where we lived. I lived in the dormitory during the school year, but this weekend I had come home so that I could study for my exam without all the noise of the dorm activity.

There was a big formal fraternity dance Friday night, and I did not get home till almost two in the morning. I was already suffering from sleep deprivation. For the last two weeks at school, I had burned the candle at both ends.

I struggled downstairs to grab a peanut butter and jelly sandwich and a glass of milk before I hit the books for the weekend. It looked like I would probably have to stay up all night Saturday studying. There was no way to get through all the material, since I blew six hours by oversleeping. I had budgeted only five to six hours of sleep a night, and I used up two nights' allocation in one swoop!

"Well, hello, Mary Sunshine," Dad grinned, as I came into the kitchen.

"I don't feel too sunny, Dad. I'm going to be up all night studying for a Western Civ exam, and this is probably the only time you'll see me. I've got to get buried in the books."

"Did I forget to tell you that there are only twenty-four hours in the day? Cutting it a little thin, aren't you?" he teased.

"I know, Dad, you've warned me but I don't seem to want to learn. I just couldn't miss the dance last night, and I know I should have studied sooner, but I just had too many things on my plate."

"Well, Kiddo, you're almost grown, but life wouldn't be so tough if you didn't try to crowd twenty-six hours into twenty-four. You'll learn one of these days, if it doesn't kill you first."

Just as Dad insisted that we take responsibility for our actions, he wanted us to understand that we could easily overcommit. Dad had frequently warned Sammy Junior and me that taking on too much at one time sets us up for failure.

Every commitment takes a chunk of time. Responsible people deliver what they promise. Overcommit and you cannot deliver. Dad's warning of "there are only twenty-four hours in the day" was the caution against taking on too much responsibility at any one time.

In order to deliver on our commitments, we must develop the judgment to know when we have unrealistic expectations. Without judgment, a responsible person can become irresponsible. Pace yourself to deliver on a promise. Better to undercommit and overdeliver than the other way around.

Yes, I knew the advice. I was just too young and eager to put it into practice. I could only hope that the candle I insisted on burning at both ends wouldn't run out of wax until *after* the Western Civ test on Monday.

PRIORITIES: Learning your limits and properly pacing yourself in life is part of becoming a responsible adult.

I dream a lot.
I do more painting when I'm not painting.
It's in the subconscious.

–Andrew Wyeth

Sleep on It
Subconscious

*D*ad told me to "sleep on it" when I complained about a tough decision. At the time, I thought it was an easy way to force me into making decisions for myself. In part, I am sure that was true. I wonder now if he knew something magic about the subconscious that he wasn't sharing.

I have noticed through the years that I have found many solutions to problems while I was asleep. The first time I noticed the real benefits was in college. During the Christmas break my freshman year, I was working on a major paper for a class in comparative literature. I had so many ideas in my head on my research topic that I just could not seem to pull all the thoughts into a cohesive theme. It seemed the more I struggled, the more confused my thinking became. I decided about midnight to take a break and have a bowl of ice cream.

As I entered the kitchen, I was surprised to see Dad still up watching a movie. It was an old Bob Hope movie, and Dad really enjoyed Hope's wit. After I got my ice cream, I sat down next to him.

I was looking for any distraction.

"Did you finish up?" he asked, bringing up a sore subject.

"No, I didn't. I've been going in circles for hours, ever since dinner. I'm no further along now than I was before we ate. I just can't seem to get all these separate facts to fit together and make any sense." I know my disgust showed in my voice.

"After you finish your ice cream, why don't you spend about five minutes glancing at all your notes and hang it up for the night. I know it sounds strange, Suzie, but you really will do better if you give it a rest and 'sleep on it.' You'll be surprised what a good night's sleep will do for you. I bet your brain will know exactly what to do if you just give it a little rest."

I took Dad's advice and sure enough the next morning the theme just flowed onto the paper. I began to wonder if there really was more to his advice than I understood. As time went on, I began to notice that when I really concentrated on a subject and got all the main points covered in my mind, if I went to bed immediately, when I awoke I seemed to have a much greater command of the subject than I did when I went to bed. I can't explain exactly how or why that seems to work. It just does.

Finding this skill is like finding a secret friend who recognizes how important something is to you, and they go get what is missing and deliver it as a surprise.

I wish I could guarantee increased wisdom every morning I wake up. The process does not seem to work like that at all. For me, my brain only works overtime on a problem if it decides I need the help. I wish I could get that help all the time and on request.

My subconscious is much more creative when it comes to innovative solutions. I wonder if some of the great inventions were created while in a sleeping state? I know that Thomas Edison kept a spot for frequent naps in his work place. I wonder if the purpose was to create or to rest?

"Sleep on it" is great advice, especially if you have an important decision to make. Overnight, the mind frequently develops a new perspective or a new approach to a problem.

SUBCONSCIOUS: Who we are is much more than the conscious part of our life. Don't underestimate the power of subconscious thought. The subconscious is free to work without the clutter of our conscious "self-talk."

Life doesn't reward quitting.
You are the only one that does that.

–Phillip C. McGraw, Ph.D.

Can't Never Could Do Nothin'

Negative Power

$\mathcal{D}$ad wasn't a Tony Robbins, a Zig Ziglar, or even a Norman Vincent Peale, but in the forties, Dad was my coach telling me "can't never could do nothing." Most of my adult life I interpreted this to mean, "Quit making excuses, Suzanne, and just go do it." For the most part, this is exactly what my dad meant.

Because of that early instruction, when I reached my twenties I refused to let my sorority sisters beg off participating in the campus spring carnival. Our sorority was well on the way to not competing because the majority had convinced themselves that we could never win against certain sororities because those sororities always won the competition. If I had accepted that, I would have to believe my one-hundred sorority sisters were not as creative and capable as any other group. That was not true, and I could not let my sorority sisters accept that negative image.

In an open meeting, I presented my belief that we could accomplish anything any other sorority could accomplish. As a result, I had to "put my money where my mouth was." I placed myself on the front line, and now I had to prove my belief. A young woman with no known musical skills was put in charge of creating a musical skit. I had the full responsibility of getting it written, cast, costumed, directed, and creating a win. I clung to the idea that it takes only one person to create a different outcome.

I had no idea how we would win; I only knew that we had to win. The only option, the only question left was how much were we willing to focus and work. The time and effort to explore the question "If we could win, what would we have to do to make that happen?" opened the door to the answers. We won second place in the Manada carnival, but we won much more as a sorority. We proved to ourselves, not others, that we could be formidable competitors if we chose to focus.

We decide how we view life. We also choose what we believe is possible, not only for ourselves but also for others. Can't is a word we hide behind. It usually means "I'm afraid." There are very few things in life that someone else has done that we cannot learn to do as well.

NEGATIVE POWER: Action is the child of a belief. Result is the child of action. No belief, no action, no results. "If you can't you must." Anthony Robbins

In short, luck's always to blame.

–Jean de La Fontaine

The Harder I Work the Luckier I Get

Luck and Persistence

*D*ad said, "If you work hard, you will get what most people call good luck." Dad's eyes literally sparkled when he said this. It was as though he were sharing an insider trade secret about his success. Dad was consistently the top salesperson for Potts-Knaur Leather Company. It was clear that he attributed his long-lived success to good old-fashioned hard work. Unsuccessful people frequently attribute success to luck or special talent. Special talent and luck are thought to be gifts rather than skills. Most people falsely believe they have been denied the opportunity to be successful. Dad considered that belief a bunch of bunk. He would retort, "Luck is great, but when I can't get any, I'll make my own luck. 'Cause the harder I work, the luckier I get."

It was April, 1986, and Dad had passed away only a few months before. I was living in Cleveland, Ohio, at the time. I was a rookie stockbroker in the downtown office of Merrill Lynch. Merrill's revenues were increasing year after year, but their expenses were out of control. In an effort to get a handle on costs, Merrill decided to launch an internal cost savings idea campaign called the Merrill Lynch Breed Apart Campaign.

As I opened my weekend mail at home, there was a promotion document, one of nine thousand mailed out. Inside the promo was the request to submit one cost savings idea to corporate. The first prize was $10,000 tax-free, and all of the top twenty contestants would receive a one-week trip for two to New York City. The winners were to be wined and dined on Wall Street as the personal guests of Dan Tully, President of Merrill Lynch. The contest was open to all employees, from the vice presidents to the Realtors of Merrill Lynch Realty.

"This was going to be fun," I thought.

Having been raised by a survivor of the Great Depression, I had been positively horrified at the waste within the corporate structure. The hard part was narrowing my suggestions down to only one. I grabbed the five-page form and began writing furiously. I was certain that my idea could save the company millions of dollars annually. Within fifteen minutes, I had completed my application and put it in the outbound mail.

The summer of 1986 would be a hard one for me. My marriage of almost twenty-five years ended abruptly. I went into a severe depression, and I moved back home to Texas to be with my widowed mother. In October 1986, I had been back to work as a stockbroker for only a week. I was starting over in Dallas with Merrill. Still consumed with grief, I was barely functioning and hoping my new branch manager would not notice. On Monday morning of my second week on the job, my branch manager walked up to my desk and said, "I need to talk to you about something pretty important."

My heart stopped. I was afraid that he knew, because of my

divorce, I was mentally functioning only 50 percent of the time. You can't possibly imagine my shock and relief when he said that I had just been named the Grand Prize Winner in the Merrill Lynch Breed Apart Campaign. I would head to New York the next week to collect my grand prize. When he left my desk, I went to the restroom and cried.

I had forgotten that I had even entered the contest the April before. I certainly needed the money. I couldn't determine if the tears were from the prospective monetary relief or because my heart was sad that I had no one to take with me to New York. There would be an awards dinner for about one hundred people. The twenty winning entrants and their spouses were to be present to receive their prizes. I was alone. I had no one to take with me. As I left the restroom, I was astonished by what followed.

All day long, one stockbroker after the other came up and congratulated me. A surprising number told me that they had a great cost-savings idea, but they never wrote it down. What was so impressive was the fact that so many of the brokers had great cost-savings ideas that they now were more than willing to bounce off the "expert."

One afternoon as I returned from lunch, a very young and high-commissioned broker came up to me. It was strange because we had never met, and several people had warned me that his arrogance was hard to take. Darren proceeded to say, "Congratulations on your luck. I would have won that prize if I had bothered to enter. I had a better idea than yours!"

Well, it hit me wrong. I was tired of life beating me up, and I wasn't interested in letting an arrogant twenty-five-year-old kid do it, too. Before I knew it, I looked him straight in the eye and said, "I'm sure lucky you and many others didn't enter, Darren. But that's what I was counting on, the fact that most people with good ideas wouldn't bother to enter. I bothered and that's why I won."

I couldn't believe I had said that. But I could hear my dad whisper, "The harder I work, the luckier I get."

LUCK AND PERSISTENCE: The most direct route to achievement is to do what others aren't willing to do. At times, it may be the only route. Achievement isn't a matter of luck; it is a matter of persistence.

Every man feels instinctively that all the beautiful sentiments in the world weigh less than a single lovely action.

–James Russell Lowell

Actions Speak Louder Than Words

Actions

*T*here was mud on his shoes, a billed cap on his head, a mischievous twinkle in his eyes, and a rose behind his back. Dad was going to tell Mom he loved her the only way he knew how.

"What are you grinning about, Sam Potter?" Mom asked, seeing Dad's face.

"It can't be the muddy feet you forgot to wipe," She teased.

"Oops. I guess I forgot that one, but I didn't forget you. I've got something for you," Dad responded, as he handed her a red rose from the backyard.

From the time Dad retired, the yard work was his job; Mom had done it for most of the years when he was on the road traveling. Mom and Dad seemed to have found a partnership, founded in love and give and take.

My daughters and I were on our annual visit with Mom and Dad during the summer. At the time, Dad had been retired for many years, and Mom and Dad were approaching fifty years of marriage.

Dad had never been comfortable with verbalizing his emotions, and I don't recall ever hearing him tell Mom that he loved her. It just wasn't Sam Potter. Mom knew how he felt, but she still longed for the verbal confirmation. Mom was not likely to hear a declaration of love from Dad, but he demonstrated his love for her through his actions almost every day of their marriage. No birthday or anniversary ever went by without a large bouquet of long-stemmed red roses—Mom's favorite. Even when he was a young man on the road traveling, Dad somehow found a way to get a Western Union telegram sent or a card delivered on every special occasion. The card or telegram was sent to take his place in the delivery of his traditional red roses. Picking Mom a special flower from the garden was a frequent and spontaneous gesture of his love and admiration.

Every time Mom got dressed up to go somewhere you could see the joy he took in her beauty. He would tell her she was a "knock out." As Mom aged, Dad never saw it. Dad never said that she was "pretty for her age;" instead he would say, "She is the most beautiful woman in the room."

As time went on and as they moved into their seventies, Dad told me that he couldn't believe how lucky he was to have her. I remember him saying, "She is the most beautiful woman in the world." Dad showed his love. He demonstrated his affection with actions. His actions spoke louder than words ever could.

Our actions in life say many things about us, and they leave a real trail of who we are and what we have become. Actions carry more weight than our words. Thought worn, the adage "talk is cheap" is true. One of the main reasons that Dad was an influential parent was that he practiced what he preached. Dad's wisdom was not preaching; it was a straightforward sharing of the rules he lived by—tested rules that he knew worked.

ACTIONS: Action defines what we really believe, and it therefore defines who we really are. "Action is character." Scott Fitzgerald

Whatever tears one may shed,
in the end one always blows one's nose.

–Heinrich Heine

They Are Just Things;
Nothing Is Worth One of Your Tears

Value of You

I was certainly old enough to know better. It wasn't as if I hadn't been warned over and over again. No matter, it was too late now! Bright red fingernail polish was spilled across the beige carpet of my bedroom. To make matters worse, the carpet was brand-new.

I watched the polish bottle tumble to the floor, as my arm brushed against the uncapped glass container. I tried in vain to catch the polish in midair. I only succeeded in causing it to spill over a wider area by putting an extra spin on the bottle. In my panic and desperation, I quickly pulled out the Cutex polish remover. I pressed hope against hope that Cutex would ride to my rescue.

Sadly, it was not meant to be.

I succeeded in smearing a bright pinkish-red blur across a larger area of brand-new beige nylon plush. Everything I tried only compounded the problem. Clearly the only thing left to do was to just break down and cry.

I threw myself across my bed and began the kind of crying that only a teenage girl would understand. Remorse turned into a mounting flood of tears and sobs. I was in the process of a sincere gut-wrenching cry when Dad came upstairs. I was so distraught that I did not hear him coming. I was totally unaware that Dad had arrived at the doorway to my bedroom and was standing there.

Somewhere, far away from my consciousness, I heard his familiar voice saying, "What's the matter, Sissy?"

He didn't say, "Oh my gosh, what have you done?" Clearly, he had seen the problem. It was too big to miss. But Dad's overriding concern was focused on my intense grief.

Hearing his voice triggered another flood of tears as I relayed every detail of my sad confession. I had ruined my brand-new carpet, even though I had been warned to be extra careful. I knew the carpet was a big expense for Mom and Dad. I had been told over and over again through the years to polish my nails in the kitchen, where there was no risk of dropping polish on the carpet. I disobeyed my mom's long-standing instructions and I ruined the carpet.

Dad lifted my chin and wiped a tear off my cheek, "They're only things, little girl, and they are not worth a single tear. We make foolish mistakes that we regret and cannot change. Now dry your eyes for me, and let's get on with the day. I love you too much to see you suffer this way. I'll tell your mom." And he left the room.

The saved money for the carpet was spent. I would spend my high school years looking at the big pink stain in my carpet every time I went in or out. Daddy and Mom were frugal. Great emphasis had always been placed on the value of the dollar. The depression of the '30s and hard times focused my dad's generation on the importance of saving and need to avoid wastefulness.

Dad rarely sent a mixed message. And this time was no different. His actions spoke to me as loudly as any words. His priorities were always clear, always consistent. It was not the love of money that drove my dad. It was the love of family and the desire to give us a better life. Dad respected money as an important element in financial survival; but Dad did not love money, he loved us.

VALUE OF YOU: There are many things in life more valuable than assets. In *this world* health, happiness, friends, and most of all family, are priceless. Things are just that—things. Part of character is the art of understanding what matters most. ". . . a man's life does not consist in the abundance of his possessions." Luke12:15

"The greatest discovery of my generation is that a human being can alter his life by altering his attitude."

–William James

WHAT WE THINK:
Attitude

In a full heart
there is room for everything,
and in an empty heart
there is room for nothing.

–Antonio Porchia

Be Grateful for What You Have
Gratitude

*I*t was my first day at Rosemont Elementary School. I was a little wide-eyed child unsure of what it would be like in a new elementary school. We had moved from Waco Street over to Montreal Avenue that meant a change from the familiar to the unfamiliar. I felt lost, unimportant, and vulnerable. I was a small fish in a sea of children. I can play the memory today as if it were a fresh video. My small and frightened third-grader eyes recorded those pictures.

There were two children I met that day whom I have never forgotten. One was a beautiful little girl named Billie, and the other was a handsome boy named Alan. I envied Billie from the first moment I saw her. She had curly, coal-black hair, perfectly brushed, falling to her shoulders. She was dressed in a cute blue-green dress with two perfectly matching little bows that held back her wonderful hair, which was parted down the middle. I don't understand why, but beautiful black hair has evoked a sense of envy in me from my earliest memories, and that preference continues to this day. That day

I wished that I could look pretty like Billie. I wanted the pretty little dress with the perfectly matched bows. This was my first experience with the emotion of envy. Every day from then on, Billie would arrive at school with little silk bows matching her outfit. She was picture perfect.

Within minutes of seeing Billie for the first time, my gaze moved across the crowded playground and found a handsome young boy, Alan. Unlike Billie, Alan did not look like a young child. His appearance seemed timeless. I thought he was only about nine, yet he was taller than most of the other children. He had the look of a handsome teenage boy, even though he was still a child. Alan had wavy white-blond hair and a flawless golden tan. He was beautiful. He was handsome. And he was crippled. Alan had polio. The crutches under each arm spoke to the severity of this dreaded disease.

The fact that Alan was so beautiful and handsome did not protect him from polio. Seeing Alan made polio real to me for the first time. Significantly, my mind identified the envy that I had experienced that morning. Envy, first felt with Billie and then with Alan. My mind moved from envy to gratitude for the first time.

God gave me a perfect lesson accentuated in its contrast and beauty with a handsome boy and pretty girl. Beautiful wavy white-blond hair and wonderful shiny black curls. Visual perfection! Yet, perfection is not always as perfect as it seems. I understood that my envy was not appropriate. Suddenly, I was grateful that I was safe, and that I did not have polio.

Through his sayings Dad had set me up to learn God's lessons. Somehow, Dad's lessons and God's wisdom worked as unseen partners in my mind.

My dad's voice was ringing inside my head: "Suzanne Pitty-Pot, you had better be grateful for what you have. You have more than most!" Whether I was begging for another scoop of ice cream or a new toy, Dad and Mom were there to rein me in and remind me of my ingratitude. I was blessed to have a single scoop. Dad was quick to focus me on what he called my "good fortune."

Children seem to possess an insatiable appetite for more. When they see something they want, they beg and plead their case. Children have no learned sense of cost and consequently can see no reason not to possess each and every thing they fancy.

We don't possess natural gratitude as a child. A child's mind doesn't understand scarcity. Gratitude is learned over time. That day on the playground, I got my first real lesson in gratitude. I believe the visual pictures in my mind have been kept clear in my memory to allow me to rerun this lesson when I forget the gifts I have been given.

GRATITUDE: The source of happiness is found in a sense of gratitude. No matter what you have, there are those with less and those with more. Gratitude evolves or does not evolve depending on which of the two children we focus on—Billie wearing her blue-green bows or Alan leaning on his crutches.

Machinery that gives us abundance
has left us in want.
Our knowledge has made us cynical,
our cleverness hard and unkind.

–Charlie Chaplin

Eating High on the Hog

Prosperity

*D*ad was eighteen when the stock market crashed in 1929, and because of that he never lost his perspective on life. Poverty and the depression gave him an appreciation for what he had, a grounding. When we were fortunate enough to have a steak, Dad would tease my brother and me about how blessed we were to be "eating high on the hog." That was his way of saying that we were eating high-class cuisine and very expensive food.

When Dad was a boy, families ate the whole animal when it was slaughtered. Everything! Fried chicken feet, hog's headcheese, brains, and pickled pigs feet—you name it! When my Dad was a boy, food scarcity was real for many American families. Refrigeration and national food distribution systems did not exist. People did not waste food the way we do today.

I can remember Mom telling us that when she was a child it was a good dinner if they had "hot stuff" or just bread and gravy. It was good because they had dinner, and they did not have to go to bed hungry with empty stomachs. "Hot stuff" was a delicious concoction of sautéed onions, hot peppers, and stewed tomatoes eaten on bread. In truth, those of us born in the '40s recall only a few hints passed down by parents about the difficulty of life during the early decades of the nineteen hundreds.

I remember visiting my grandmother, Ginny Ma, and her frying chicken for Sunday dinner. There on the table was the fried chicken, including the fried feet. I don't remember what happened to the feet. I know I sure did not eat them!

If it were not for some faded recollections from my own childhood, I would have no sense of the difficulty experienced during the Depression. When I was a child, we raised chickens in the backyard, and I watched in child-stricken horror as the hens ran in circles long after their necks were wrung. I watched Dad dip the freshly killed chickens in boiling water before plucking off the feathers.

In the late forties, no one locked the doors, and people knew their neighbors. Food in the forties and fifties was simple, country food. We ate dried beans of all kinds. It was a major source of our protein. Eating out was neither affordable nor available, and most households used an icebox; refrigerators would come later. Grocery distribution was not yet well established, so many of the foods we ate were grown and eaten locally. Getting artichokes or avocados from California was unheard of.

My childhood was a more prosperous time than that which my parents experienced, yet my childhood seems light years away from the affluence of today. Technology has changed so much so quickly. It is difficult to stay connected to our own past, much less that of a prior generation.

When Dad said we were eating "high on the hog," it is hard to imagine the memories that he had stored. I have no idea what

foods made up the diet for my mom or my dad when they were children. I do know that Dad's upbringing did not give him much of a
chance to "eat high on the hog."

PROSPERITY: We have so much abundance in our country. It
is easy to forget that our abundance is a blessing of this country and
this generation, and it came from the hard work and commitment of
our nation. As a nation, we share in the wealth and abundance that
we all create. We eat "high on the hog" only because as a country we
have made the hog available.

The future ain't what it used to be.

–Yogi Berra

There Is No Time Like the Present

Procrastination

*T*he inevitable teenage stalls and delays in washing the dishes, cleaning the bathroom, sweeping the floor, picking up clothes, or doing homework were accompanied either by the prod "there is no time like the present" or another of Dad's favorites, "never put off till tomorrow what you can do today."

I am certain that you never put anything off like I did.

Even though the chores were distasteful and dreaded, it never changed the fact that they were not going to get done until I did them. Putting them off not only dragged out the inevitable, but it aggravated, at a minimum, three people. It aggravated Mom because the chores were not done and the house was a mess. It aggravated me because the chore would not go away. It aggravated Dad because the two women in the house were not at peace.

When Dad said, "There is no time like the present," he was giving me more wisdom than a lesson in procrastination.

As I wrote Dad's eulogy in 1986, I realized that Dad's legacy was the ability to enjoy each day, one at a time. To him life was about the day at hand and there was "no time like the present." His words that nudged me into action as a teenager exposed a new meaning to me in adulthood. Because of Dad's example, I began to see a deeper relevance in priorities. His coaching on procrastination evolved into a lesson on priorities.

Today is the priority. Today is where all the joy is experienced or lost forever. Today is the opportunity, not tomorrow. All of life and joy are in the now, the moment at hand.

Today I find myself asking, "how can I be Sam Potter's daughter, and not have learned the most fundamental lesson he tried to teach me?" That lesson was truly, there is no time like the present!

PROCRASTINATION: Procrastination creates more stress in life than just rolling up your sleeves and getting the job done. "There is no time like the present" has a deeper wisdom: Live life in the moment; fully value the time at hand. There is no more costly a procrastination than delaying today's joys till tomorrow.

Life is what's happening while
we're busy making other plans.

Every Day I Get Up, It Is a Good Day

Perspective

*T*he first time I heard Dad say this he was turning sixty. I had been living out of state and was home with my children for a two-week summer visit. It was early one morning, and only Dad and I were up. The coffee was perking, and we sat down at the kitchen table to wait for it to finish so that we could enjoy the first cup of the day. The smell of the coffee was wonderful, and as I wondered how much longer it would take to finish perking, out of the blue Dad said, "You know, Suzie, people are always saying 'Have a good day,' and most of them don't even know what that means. Suz, every day I get up, it's a good day." I didn't even ask why he said what he did. I just listened.

Dad clearly felt the sense of finality that comes all too soon in old age. I remember the haunting melancholy that engulfed me when I first heard Peggy Lee's song, *Is That All There Is?* That same sadness flooded over me. I was sad inside, and yet, Dad was not. I was afraid to speak; the thought of losing Mom or Dad was unbearable. I could

What We Think: Attitude 137

feel my fear. At the same time, I could feel Dad's calm.

Dad began to speak frankly about many of his friends who were having emotional crises as they aged. Many were afraid of dying. Dad said he was not afraid. He said that he had a good life and just enjoyed every day as it came. We never spoke about how he felt other than to say that he was not going to waste time worrying. He gave me a big grin and jumped up to pour the coffee. As he handed me my hot cup, he said, "Yep, every day I get up, it's a good day."

I knew what Dad meant. He had said it many times before: "Life is a gift, and it is not to be wasted on things you can't do anything about. Life is about choices; you can either appreciate it or not." This philosophy was nothing new for Dad. He decided as a very young man to enjoy the gift of each day, one day at a time. Worrying was not on his agenda.

After the girls and I left Dallas to return to Tampa, I thought a lot about what Dad had said. His perspective made me question how well I was doing in my appreciation of "This is the day the Lord has made, let us rejoice and be glad in it." Dad had always shown appreciation for the moment throughout his whole life. His light-hearted attitude toward the gift of one more day of life was full of unspoken wisdom. Every day is precious and to be relished. He viewed each day as the gift it truly is. Many times I feel a cloud of guilt when I think of all the days I've wasted because I did not appreciate the gift I had. Simple appreciation is an art.

PERSPECTIVE: Life is a precious gift, and we need to be grateful and appreciate fully each day as it is given.

I ain't done bad for an old lady.

–Grandma Moses

If You Think Getting Old Is Bad, It Sure Beats the Alternative

Aging

*M*om was clearly in a huff.

It was 1985, and I was in Dallas for another annual visit. I wasn't fully unpacked before Mom made clear that her displeasure was directed at Dad's lack of discretion. "He told *everyone* in the doctor's office that I got social security!" she fumed.

I had to mentally fill in the facts. Of course she got social security. I knew Mom was born in 1913, although she would have been horrified that I knew the real date of her birth. Of course she would be furious with Dad for letting anyone know that she was no longer a "spring chicken."

Mom and Dad had never fought in fifty years of marriage, but Dad had clearly stepped into an area where no man dared to go. Dad should have known that Mom would be unforgiving. He had seen Mom change doctors just because they pressed the issue when she told them that her age was none of their business.

It would have been a useless exercise for me to attempt to convince Mom that she should be proud of her age. I knew better! I just sympathized and assured her that Dad's slip was unintentional. I was sure he would never do it again!

When I was young, age seemed irrelevant. It no longer seems so. Even in her youth, my mom was consumed with the unwillingness to recognize the aging process. One of my earliest memories of her was her refusal to tell her age. Jack Benny stopped the clock at age thirty-nine. Mom, a Benny contemporary, stopped the clock at thirty-five. As time passed, it was as if by not telling someone her age, a new reality was created. For Mom, the saying that "time waits for no man" only applied to men! Old Father Time would never be so unobliging to a lady.

To the day my mother died, she was protective of her age. As far as she was concerned, it was nobody's business how old she was. Dad, on the other hand, always Mom's polar opposite, relished the fact that he had been gifted with another year of life. The older Dad got, the more appreciative he became of each additional day. Almost every visit, from the time I married in 1963 until he died in 1986, he would say, "If you think getting old is bad, it sure beats the alternative." Generally, he would follow that saying with a hearty laugh, and we would giggle knowingly together.

Perhaps, this saying was the best way Dad had to dislodge my mom's fear of aging. But it was my perception that this particular saying was more a description of Dad's philosophy than an effort to instruct Mom.

Dad's view of life was more about the inner experience than the outer experience. He totally embraced the principle that negative thinking can rob life of its joy. By focusing on the wrong thing, we create fear and miss the pleasures of daily living. Dad understood that life could offer pleasure in the moment at any and all ages. Dad did not fear aging; he relished it.

In fairness to Mom, women have historically been judged and valued by their beauty. Time erodes exterior beauty. My mother was a very beautiful woman, and she saw time as her enemy. My dad was not a physically attractive man, and for him, time did not hold the same threat.

Regardless of Dad's intent, I can see his belief assert itself in my willingness to admit my age. Like my dad, I will not let Father Time or society dictate life's pleasures. To accept aging as undesirable is to believe that life after a certain point is worthless. God gives us our time on earth. He never gives a worthless gift. It is our use of that time that creates our experience.

AGING: To fear aging is an irrational fear. The real fear is to lose the zest for new life experiences.

Good timber does not grow with ease;
the stronger the wind, the stronger the trees.

-J. Willard Marriott

When It Rains, It Pours

Bad Times

*A*fter dinner Mom looked at Dad and said, "I'm really worried about the Osters, Jimmie especially. Johnny's company is laying people off, and he is worried that he will be next. All that comes on top of Jimmie's breast cancer diagnosis. I don't know what to do to help them through this."

We all knew Mom was really worried about Jimmie's upcoming mastectomy. In the '50s, people didn't know much about breast cancer except that women generally died from it. Since Mom's teenage years, Jimmie had been one of her best friends.

Dad said, "Sweetheart, try not to worry about something you can't change. Doctors are getting better at this every day. I know it feels like bad things are coming at the Osters from all sides. Life seems to be predictable like that, 'When it rains, it pours.' The best thing I know to do is to remember that most storms rain themselves out and the skies clear up. Besides, I have a hunch that Jimmie is just too tough to let cancer get the better of her."

Dad was right. Johnny did not lose his job after all. Even though Jimmie had a massive mastectomy, she seemed to go on with her life with renewed gusto and humor. Jimmie was tough! She beat the odds and ultimately outlived both my mom and my dad. As I grew up, it was comforting to watch the first cancer patient I ever knew, beat the disease decade after decade.

There are times in our life that we need sympathy and courage. Life has inexplicable moments when pain or disaster seem to keep assailing a person over and over again. There are other times when we just need a friendly word of support, acknowledging that we are running into repeated setbacks. Either way, this proverb was how Dad expressed support. He let us know that he knew times were hard.

The beauty of this powerful metaphor is that it not only conveyed gentle support in a time of need, it also delivered subtle encouragement—it will stop raining, and at some point, the sun will shine again.

This simple saying began when I was young. By the time I was old enough to encounter bigger periods of hard times, Dad had programmed me to know that no matter how painful life became, the pain, just like the rainstorm, would pass inevitably. Hopefully, the parenting we received as children supports our life journey; otherwise, we must find ways to support ourselves. Dad blessed me with sympathetic imagery from my childhood. That imagery has sustained me.

BAD TIMES: Many periods of life contain one bad event after the other. Bad times do finally end and sunshine returns to our lives. Look forward to a better future. Nothing in this life lasts forever.

There are no hopeless situations—
only people who are hopeless about them.

–Dinah Shore

This, Too, Shall Pass Away

Pain

I was just thirteen and my heart was broken. First love is so painful, and the first heartbreak is devastating. It must have been hard for my father to watch his little girl spend hours on end listening to songs about unchanging love and sitting alone, crying her heart out. I still remember the weeping and the pain. The grief seemed insurmountable. I knew I would never quit feeling the pain of loss.

Joy's extreme highs and pain's terrible lows are part of being a teen. How can anyone so young see the end and understand the evolution of life's first misery?

Dad must have felt helpless, fearful, and out of his element. How does a tough man, taught by his elders not to cry, handle his little girl, whose heart is breaking and whose face is covered in an unending stream of tears? Sadness and heavy emotions were not areas of life that Daddy visited voluntarily. If he were to help his little girl, he had to go there.

I remember Dad coming into the living room. All the lights were out except a strange red bulb that gave a reddish hue to the dim room. I was playing a popular but painful song on our 45 rpm record player. The song was *Hurt*. It verbalized all my pain and let me visit it each time I replayed it.

The fact that Dad came into the living room that day was in itself unusual. He respected the privacy that we needed as growing teens. When he came in, he did not say much. He told me that he loved me, and that as much as I hurt I needed to believe that he knew the truth. He told me he would always tell me the truth. I believed in my dad's love, and I knew he had always been truthful. Dad said he loved me and always would no matter what, and that no matter how big the hurt, time would slowly heal it. As he left the room with my music playing and the tears slowing, he turned and said, "this, too, shall pass away." Dad's words reminded me of a song that was popular in the '50s. The phrase "this, too, shall pass away" was part of the song's title. It was his quiet way of replacing a sad song, *Hurt*, with another song. The new song promised healing.

It was many years before the feelings of anguish left, and as the years moved on the pain did pass. There is something very special about our youth. As we reach out and experience feelings for others for the first time, we are very vulnerable. The highs are like a roller coaster at its crest, and the lows are like huge waves crashing against tall rocks. The wisdom to help a teen feel the hope of tomorrow despite emotional lows is the challenge of parenting.

Had I not known my dad would always love me, unconditionally, without strings, where would I have found meaning? If I had not known that he always told me the truth, how could I have believed that life would get better? Many years later, after Dad had died, I went through another pain. But his lessons were still there, helping me see beyond the pain to tomorrow.

PAIN: Time dulls all pain and fades all pleasure. The promise of tomorrow will eventually outweigh the pain of yesterday.

We either make ourselves happy or miserable.
The amount of work is the same.

–Carlos Castaneda

Misery Loves Company

Misery

$\mathcal{A}$s I opened the front door, I could smell the vegetable soup cooking. I knew Dad must be in the kitchen. No one made better soup than Dad. It was hot and spicy, and it could cause you to break out in a sweat just from eating it.

As expected, Dad was sitting at the kitchen table, taking a load off his feet. By the look of the counter, he had just finished peeling carrots and potatoes. When I walked in, I seemed to catch him by surprise. Dad seemed somber.

"What's the matter, Dad? You look so serious."

"Nothing much, Suzie. I was just thinking about Fred and Johnnie Lorenz."

"What's going on, Dad, you don't look as happy as usual?" I was sensing his concern.

"Suz, I don't know if you remember, but Fred and Johnnie lost their only child, a girl, when she was killed in a car wreck. She was barely twenty and Johnnie has never really gotten over it, and that was over twenty-five years ago."

"I don't understand, Dad. What does that have to do with now?" I asked, trying to figure out where he was headed.

"Well, Suzie, you know Fred is a cutup and full of fun and laughter. He has always tried to create a happy life for Johnnie and himself over the years. Fred retired from the carpet business last year, and things have gotten frustrating for him. Johnnie is so busy being miserable that it is dragging him down. Finally, he just had to tell her that with the years he's got left he's going to be happy, and he'd like her to be happy, too.

"He just flat told her 'Johnnie, misery loves company and you keep choosing misery for yourself year after year, and you want to have me share that misery with you. It has been twenty-five years, and it is way past time for us to get on with the joy of living. I'm tired of misery, and if you want to choose happiness I'll keep you company; but if you want to keep complaining and making life miserable, you're going to have to find someone else to keep you company.'

"It's hard, Suzie, but Fred is right, misery does love company, and it is an emotion that should never be allowed to unpack and move in for a permanent stay. Johnny converted her grief to misery years ago, and she just got comfortable there and never moved on.

"They'll work it out. Fred is too full of life to let Johnnie continue. He's never forced her to take action before, but now he has. I know Johnnie; she's sweet but emotionally lazy. Johnnie has never had to change or do much of anything until now. She will though, and they'll both be better for it."

MISERY: In what pattern of behavior are we engaged? Approach life's pains with caution. If we focus all our energy on these, we miss the positives life offers. Until we focus attention toward the positives, we cannot and will not develop a plan to move on.

Self-pity dries up
our sympathy for others.

–Mason Cooley

Quit Crying Over Spilt Milk

Self-Pity

*C*learly, I needed to cry. An avalanche of tears was answering the need. I was seven and a half months pregnant, and this had been a terrible week.

Monday started with a distraction while cooking dinner. I was frying French fries and left them for a few minutes. Bad mistake! The kitchen cabinets caught on fire.

On Wednesday, our old washer got out of balance, and before I could stop it, it had ripped up two linoleum tiles in the utility room.

Today was Saturday. Bad things always happen in threes.

I had just gone to the refrigerator to pour some milk for my little girl, Kristy, and the full gallon jug slipped from my hand. The glass container exploded as it hit the floor. Glass and milk covered the entire kitchen. Instant tears followed. I was so big and so fat and so tired. How was I going to clean all this up?

I couldn't mop it because of all the glass. I couldn't bend over to pick up the glass because I was as big as a house. As I sobbed, I sat down in despair. I was alone and I was going to have to deal with this mess, pregnant or not. As I wiped away the tears and tried to lean across the floor while throwing down paper towels, I began to laugh. I could hear my voice actually saying, "This must be that spilt milk that Dad was always telling me not to cry over!"

I was so mad at myself for not holding onto the jug handle tighter. As I berated myself, I finally recognized that my attitude didn't change anything.

Dad always said that there was no point in crying over spilt milk. He knew Sammy Junior and I were going to make mistakes in our lives, and that we would probably be harder on ourselves than anyone else. Dad just wanted us to understand that if we can't change things, then quit agonizing and get on with life. The longer we spend looking backward and mourning over things that cannot be changed, the more we waste the life at hand.

While this is great advice, some things in life are harder to get over than others. Sometimes doing what needs to be done is not as easy as it sounds. When there is a great deal of emotional pain, it is exceptionally hard to move on. But the longer we focus on the spilt milk, the less time we have for living.

I may sound brave and philosophical now, but as soon as I cleaned up the glass and milk, I called Mom and said: " Mom? I need to cry over some spilt milk!"

SELF-PITY: Time wasted on worrying about things that cannot be changed takes time away from working on things that can.

*I've been on a calendar
but never on time.*

–Marilyn Monroe

Dollar Waiting on a Dime

Value of Family

"Dollar waiting on a dime!" Dad was ready to go and Mom was not. It was no more complicated than that. There was no need to say "hurry up." We all knew Dad was the "dollar" and Mom was the "dime."

For most of my life, I never thought about what the saying really meant. I assumed that I knew. As I grew and learned, I realized that so many of the things my father laughingly threw out in jest were really thought-provoking ideas with multiple layers of meaning.

A "dollar waiting on a dime" wasn't just about Mom and Dad; on another level, the saying was about value and time. The expression struck at the heart of foolish behavior when it came to allocating life's greatest assets—time and money.

Dad was the breadwinner in our family. When Mom kept him waiting and waiting and waiting for her to get dressed, Dad would tease her by calling out "dollar waiting on a dime." It was my father's way of coaxing Mom to "get a move on" so they would not be late.

In spite of the teasing, Dad was patient; it was always clear the "dollar" deeply loved the "dime."

There was only one day in all the decades of my parents' marriage that I remember the "dollar" not waiting on the "dime." It was Saturday, November 23, 1963, a day most historians will remember as the day after President John F. Kennedy was shot in Dallas, Texas. For me, it was an emotion-filled day following an emotional and chaotic assassination on Friday. I had been looking forward to a beautiful and sunny forecast for the November weekend. A perfect day for a wedding! November 23 was my wedding day. Things were certainly emotional. I was supposed to marry in Saint Thomas Aquinas Catholic Church at 6:30 P.M. Saturday. In the shock of the assassination, I was not even sure that the Catholic Church would go forward with any weddings. John F. Kennedy was the first Catholic president ever elected in the United States. He was not only assassinated in Dallas, but he was the first U.S. President assassinated in modern times.

I was so overwhelmed with the tears and the stress of the assassination that I barely remember the events that followed. I was Dad's only little girl. I was getting married; it was a first for him also. The schedule called for me to arrive at the church at 4:30 P.M., with my wedding dress in tow. I was to dress at the church, and it was at least an hour's drive across town. I remember all the jokes leading up to the wedding day about how slow Mom was when it came to getting dressed, and how she never seemed to relate to a time schedule.

My wedding day was the one day that we had to be on time. That Saturday morning, things were moving at a furious pace. There was so much to do and so little time. My dad never liked to be late, and this event was more important than anything else we as a family had ever done. Prior tardiness on Mom's account had never before been a critical issue. In the past, Dad's love for Mom and his innate patience allowed him to calmly wait each time they went anywhere. Dad's method to speed Mom along was his vocal "dollar waiting on a dime," accompanied by the quiet snickering of my brother, Sammy Junior, and me.

This day my emotions were numb, my eyes felt glazed, and nothing seemed real. Everything was a slow-moving dream. Dad looked concerned and clearly felt the weight of the moment. He knew he would have to take control of the time.

Waiting on Mom and nudging her along started early in the day. Dad hoped that an early start would give Mom plenty of time so that we could all go to the church together. I am sure rushing felt foolish to Mom as she started to dress at two o'clock for a six-thirty wedding. Before I knew it, I had showered, put on my makeup, packed my bag, and put on an outfit to wear over to the church. At three o'clock, Dad and Sammy Junior showed up at my door in their beautiful suits and ties for the wedding. I was ready, but I could tell by Dad's tense look that Mom was more than thirty minutes away from being ready. Our drop-dead time to leave the house was three-thirty. Dad, Sammy Junior, and I went downstairs in an effort to not make Mom more nervous. We knew full well from past experience that when she got nervous, she got slower. For the three of us, the thirty minutes dragged on like an eternity, but for Mom, it evidently went like a flash. When we all converged to tell her we had to go NOW, she seemed no further along than when we had left her thirty minutes before.

Daddy, Sammy Junior, and I went downstairs for the second time. For a few minutes, we just stood and stared blankly at one another, unsure of what to do. Suddenly, Dad turned and told Sammy Junior to drive Mom to the church whenever she got ready, and that he hoped they would make it by six-thirty in time for her to be ushered down the aisle as the mother of the bride. Dad took the keys to the other car, and we were off. No anger; just this once the "dollar" could not wait on the "dime." We laughed all the way to the church, thinking how predictable it all was. Mom did make it just in time for the processional.

VALUE OF FAMILY: The market place may value our time in dollars, but love and family are not measured in the market place; they are weighed in the heart. In life's hierarchy, human relationships are the greater wealth.

*The whole value of time
is knowing what to do with it.*

–Ralph Waldo Emerdon

First Time Browned
Is the Best Time Browned

Best Time

*A*s my dad moved into his late forties, he started to cook. Initially, it was just big pots of spicy-hot vegetable soup. As time went on, steak preparation became a Daddy-only job. Somehow, it just evolved until Dad and Mom reversed their roles. Mom stopped cooking very much, and Dad began cooking all of the time.

Dad was a great cook, not a gourmet chef, but an unbeatable Southern-style home-cooking cook. If Dad had not been so successful in business, he could have made a living as a short-order cook. He would have filled up any truck stop.

As time passed, it became harder and harder for Dad to come into a kitchen and not be involved. If he was visiting while cooking was under way, he just had to lift a lid and stir the pot. Frequently, as his need for participation rose, he would have to ask if the pot needed anything. Translation: "Do you want me to taste it and tell you what it needs?"

Dad enjoyed cooking almost as much as he enjoyed eating.

He fought a constant battle with his waistline all of his adult life, but his battle was half-hearted at best.

One morning Mom and Dad came over for breakfast with the girls and me. By this time, Dad had been retired from selling for several years. My three girls were always excited when their grandparents, Honey and Gigi, visited. I don't remember the occasion for the early visit, but pancakes were on my mind. I made the batter from scratch, and I started to cook, while Dad sat at the kitchen table drinking his hot coffee.

Dad, in his usual form, felt the itch to have his hand in the "fixins." I poured the batter onto the hot griddle. I watched the bubbles start to form in the hot batter, and I stood at the stove with a spatula in my hand waiting to turn the pancakes. Dad silently slipped up behind me, and all of a sudden he leaned his smiling, sweet face around my right shoulder as he quickly uttered his cooking tip. "First time browned is the best time browned," he said, then winked and slid away, back to his newspaper and coffee.

I am laughing as I write, because I knew he just could not resist the impulse to do some of the cooking! Even that morning, the more I thought about what he said and the way he said it, the more I laughed. How did he know that about pancakes? Where could he have gotten that idea? It was the first time I had ever thought about turning pancakes, but Dad was right. Pancakes look better and taste better with only one turn on the griddle.

This winter, while on a ski trip to Colorado, I went into the City Market, along with all the other skiers to stock the condo kitchen for our stay. The passing decades hadn't diminished my fondness for pancakes. A small package of add-water-only pancake mix caught my eye. For a mere sixty-nine cents, I could buy a package of mix and add just enough water to make one or two pancakes each morning. One package could be strung out for two of us over the whole week because the mix did not require eggs and milk like most mixes do. If eggs are required, it is not possible to make the batter for a small number of pancakes. How do you halve or quarter an egg? If you make all the batter at one time, it does not keep well, even if you refrigerate it. Instantly, I thought to myself, "This will be perfect, practical, and cheap."

The mix was a brand I had never seen, Krusteaz Buttermilk Complete Pancake Mix/Just Add Water. While trying to decide whether or not to take the plunge and buy an unknown brand on something as important as "my" pancakes, I turned the package over to read the instructions. It was all over. SOLD! The last step in the three-step process on the back of the package read:

> 3. COOK pancakes 1–11/4 minutes per side,
> or until golden brown, **turning only once**.

The words "turning only once" spun my mind backward in time, and Dad's soft blue eyes once again were looking into mine, and I could feel his presence as I lovingly remembered, "first time browned, is the best time browned." Tears began to fill my eyes as I recognized, thirty years later, that I was being reminded of Dad's wisdom from the back of a package of pancake mix. I grabbed the package and checked out.

The pancakes were great. I went back to the City Market and bought a box to bring home. I told myself it was because they were good, and I could make just enough batter for one or two pancakes at a time. I knew the truth as I picked up that homebound box. I bought it for the memories it stirred. Even as I grabbed the Krusteaz Buttermilk Complete Pancake Mix, a sense of dread went through me. I dreaded the time when it would be all gone. I would no longer have the box that confirmed my dad's wisdom and brought his warm presence.

BEST TIME: When and how things are done is as important as what is done. There is a best time to learn, earn, marry, and have children. Pay personal attention to the timing of the big things in your life, as well as the small.

Whoever is in a hurry shows that the thing
he is about is too big for him.

—4th Earl of Chesterfield

The Hurrieder I Go, the Behinder I Get

Work and Pace

*I*t would not have occurred to Dad to just say, "Slow down." Telling a child to slow down is a direct command; it does not explain the reason for the suggestion. Dad's style not only brought fun to the interaction, but more often than not his words of wisdom clarified the undesirable end result. These words were a silly reminder that most things don't go better or faster by trying to rush through them.

As a teen, I always seemed to be in a tizzy. Rushing here and there, starting multiple projects and bouncing like a ball back and forth between. When we rush the natural process of a task, we aggravate our ability to get the job done. Stress and mental confusion set in and, ultimately, the task takes longer than it should have taken. Dad used this phrase to tell me to pace myself and be patient.

Teenagers frequently tune out parental advice, and I'm sure I would have done so as well if Dad had given me the opportunity. He didn't hand out advice, so I couldn't hand it back. Instead, he gave quick and concise life observations.

Dad would never have been so overt as to observe that my "haste" was making a lot of "waste." Instead, he used "the hurrieder I go, the behinder I get" and engaged the first person "I." Dad enrolled himself in like behavior and predicted his own personal result of getting further behind. It took no large leap of logic on my part to conclude that if Dad got behind by rushing too fast, then maybe I would also. Dad preferred this saying to the tame version, "haste makes waste." Both proverbs coach the same lesson, but Dad's version captured my attention and permanently fixed it in my heart and head. Every now and then, I catch my brain repeating the cautionary lesson "the hurrieder I go, the behinder I get."

WORK AND PACE: Some things cannot be rushed. If you try to rush a task, it often takes more time, not less. The best teaching is often not instruction but observation.

Patience and tenacity of purpose are worth
more than twice their weight of cleverness.

–Thomas Henry Huxley

Patience Is a Virtue
Waiting

$\mathcal{D}$ad loved to go fishing. Fishing is definitely a test of patience. I recall the hot, hot summers when we would take a little metal flat-bottom boat with a small horsepower motor out on McKinney Club Lake. Dad would steer the tiny boat into a quiet cove, where the only noise was an occasional splat of a bass or bream flipping out of the water.

Sometimes after we anchored and Dad baited our hooks, a dragonfly's noisy wings would startle and frighten me. I was afraid of everything as a kid. I was afraid to touch minnows or worms. I was terrified of spiders and dragonflies. I had been stung more than once in the middle of the night by a scorpion.

Scorpion stings in the home were not that uncommon in Texas during the '40s. The sight of a big, black, furry tarantula in the front yard or occasionally inside was also unnervingly common. Needless to say, I had a grounded fear. Just to be on the safe side, I choose to fear *all* insects.

As we sat in the stifling hundred-degree heat without even the slightest breeze, the beads of perspiration began to form and run down our scalps. We had been taught to quietly watch the cork and yank the hook if and when the cork went under. This was an exercise in patience and persistence. Patience and absolute silence were required to be a good fisherman. If you talked too much, or were too loud, you scared off the fish. Patience caught fish.

For me, fishing was dull and I was quickly bored. I thought nothing was happening. In reality, things were happening, while I learned to wait. The fish were moving under the water, while I sat still. Because I could not see what was happening, I believed nothing was happening.

Years later, when I reentered the job market after a sixteen-year absence, Dad's lessons on patience were put to the test. I had just moved to Florida, and in '81 I decided that I wanted to sell real estate. FHA and VA mortgages were at 17.5 percent, and the real estate market wasn't dying; it was dead. It took a lot of patience and personal belief to weather that market and build my business. If Dad had not taught me patience and tenacity, I'm sure I would have given up too soon.

I've found that life is a lot like fishing. Many times we do not see what is going on, and because we cannot see it we believe nothing is happening. God is always under us, and just like the water we cannot always see what is happening, but something is going on unseen. Faith in our course of action generates the patience to wait for our actions to produce results.

WAITING: Some things in life just require more time than we think they should. Just by hanging on and moving forward, success moves up and we find that it is, suddenly, just around the corner.

We never really know what stupid is
until we have experimented on ourselves.

–Paul Gauguin

There's No Explaining Stupid

Foolish Behavior

*M*amaw was coming to visit! Mamaw was my great grandmother from Waco, Texas, and the sweetest and the spryest old lady you would ever want to meet.

Annie Jones, my "Mamaw," grew up in the late 1800s in Texas. Annie ran a boarding house for the railroad traffic and had been married to someone my mom referred to as "Big Daddy." Mamaw raised her three daughters and two sons pretty much on her own. Mamaw's oldest daughter, Ora Mae, married Abner Gressett and by the time she was seventeen, she gave birth to my mom. The marriage was over almost as soon as it started. Mamaw did most of Mom's parenting, with different aunts and uncles pitching in. Ora Mae wasn't finished sowing her wild oats, and as a result Mom never had her need for a traditional mom and dad fulfilled.

I remember Mamaw in her sixties, riding in from Waco on the Greyhound bus for a visit. Her small, navy-blue straw hat with a thin brim and tiny veil sat tilted off to the left, as if to tell the world that this ole girl wasn't finished, yet. Her curly hair had that funny purple, blue-gray color that marked her as an "old lady."

Mamaw was addicted to her snuff. She was embarrassed by the habit, so she kept a tin can hidden close by for a periodic deposit. Dad couldn't resist, and he teased her about it. He'd say, "Annie, we all know where the can is. You don't have to hide it. You're just liable to lose it if you keep stashing it away like that."

It was a cold spring weekend when she came to visit us. We lived in our first home on Waco Street in Dallas at that time. The house was a small two-bedroom, one-bath home. The second bed-room was no more than an enlarged converted sleeping porch. Sammy Junior and I had twin beds. We shared the room with a play-ful hamster recently acquired as the family pet. Everyone knew that a hamster was little more than a glorified rat. Mom could tolerate the idea of a hamster, whereas a rat was unthinkable.

Mamaw was assigned Sammy Junior's twin bed for the night. Her long, thin, nylon blue floral print dress was hung on a nail in the wall with her granny lace-up shoes on the bare floor.

The next morning Mamaw let out a screeching shout: "What's happened? What happened to my dress?" Frantically, we all came running. Dad, Mom, Sammy Junior, and I stared in utter amazement. The whole bottom half of Mamaw's skirt was eaten away. The bottom of her dress looked like the manila paper snowflakes that preschool-ers cut out at Christmas.

All of a sudden, Dad's mind solved the mystery, and he let out a howl of laughter. I remember being half asleep and asking what happened. About that time Mamaw screamed again as she accused the culprit, "It's a mouse, a mouse! Get rid of it! Get rid of it! It's a mouse that did it."

Dad was laughing so hard that all he could finally utter was "We'll get you another dress, Mamaw. The hamster was just doing what hamsters do. But as for hanging your dress over his cage, well, he paused and laughed. As he hugged her, he said, "Sometimes, there's just no explaining stupid."

"Someone" had hung Mamaw's dress with the hem gently draped over the hamster cage. Not the cleverest of moves for sure. What a feast! And from the looks of things, the feast lasted the better part of the night. No one ever admitted hanging the dress on the nail.

This was my first recollection of "there's no explaining stupid." Over the years, Dad used this phrase often. Dad's expression had nothing to do with IQ. This was about doing something that if you had thought about it, you would have known better! There is a vast difference between doing stupid things and being stupid. Dad used these words to refer to an act that created a negative and unanticipated result. This expression was designed to teach Sammy Junior and me to look forward to the consequences of our actions.

Implicit in Dad's saying was the fact that with a small amount of thought the negative results could be avoided. If some of the negative results in life are avoidable, then it is foolish and stupid not to think first.

FOOLISH BEHAVIOR: Forethought avoids most mistakes. "There's no explaining stupid" warns us not to get mentally lazy. We must think before we act, even in small decisions. Results are the consequences of actions. Actions are the by-product of thought or the lack thereof.

If You Want Something Done Halfway Send a Kid To Do It.
If You Want Something Not Done at All Send Two.

Children and Joy

*I*t was Friday afternoon, and Dad was home early for the weekend. I had just gotten home from junior high school, and Sammy Jr. was due home any minute from Rosemont Elementary. When I opened the front door, my mouth started watering! I could smell Mom's Italian spaghetti and meatballs cooking on the stove. There was nothing I would rather have than a big plate of Mom's spaghetti. Dad and Mom were in the kitchen. Dad was sipping a bourbon and Coke, and Mom was drinking a big glass of iced tea.

"Yummy, when can we eat?" I was already starving.

"Pretty soon! Sammy Junior should be home with the French bread any second. I told him to stop at Schindler's Bakery on the way home and get us a large loaf of French bread. It comes out of the oven about the same time school lets out. I just hope he doesn't eat the whole loaf before he gets home, or we'll be out of luck. Most of the time at least a half a loaf makes it in the door." Mom grinned and started the salad.

About that time, Dad said, "I hope Sammy Junior is riding his bike home alone and not with a friend."

Nosy me piped up, "Why, Daddy?"

"Well, Sissy, —if you want something done halfway, send a kid to do it. If you want something not done at all, send two! So if we want to have any garlic bread, we better hope he's alone."

Mom and I giggled. It had been a long time since either one of us had heard Dad use this saying. It always caught us off guard. No matter how many times we heard it, it always sounded funny. Dad saw fun in everything, and he was just pushing our buttons until the "bread messenger" arrived.

This saying was Dad's favorite observation about children. He found humor in the predictability of kids. Children are full of discovery and mischief, and Dad enjoyed their sense of freedom. I don't think Dad even got mad the time when Sammy Junior caught the back fence on fire. Sammy Junior accomplished that "accident" by himself; it is scary to think about how much more mischief might have occurred if he had had the benefit of an accomplice!

Children don't have an urgent agenda; they just are. They don't have priority lists and timelines. A single child may be lackadaisical, but put two or more children together and their fun-loving, discovery-filled, mischievous natures add to more than just one plus one.

As we sat in the kitchen talking, Sammy Junior stormed in, slung his backpack on the table, a half-mangled loaf of French bread protruding from the top.

"Hi, Dad," Sammy Junior grinned. "I got us a hot loaf from Schindler's."

"It looks like you've already had your half. This is enough for me, but what are the rest of you going to eat?" Dad was baiting us again.

"Dad, I rode as fast as I could to get here. As soon as I put that hot loaf in my backpack, the smell started to get to me. I tried to wait, but before I knew it I was reaching over my shoulder and pulling off a piece of bread. It was so good that once I got started I couldn't stop. If I didn't ride fast, there would be nothing left!"

"What can I say, Bubba? If you want something done halfway, send a kid to do it. If you want something not done at all, send two. I'm just grateful you didn't have a pal along for the ride. Now let's fix us some grub before what's left of that bread gets cold!"

CHILDREN AND JOY: Kids focus on the joy, not the job. Adults focus on the job, not the joy. Who should be the teacher?

If it were not for the company of fools,
a witty man would often
be greatly at a loss.

–François, Duc de La Rochefoucauld

You're Sure Smarter than You Look

Fun

"**Y**ou old son-of-a-gun! You've been stealing my tomatoes!" Jim Craig bellowed as he broke up in laughter. Dad's quick retort was, " You're sure smarter than you look."

The long, intricate game that Dad was playing had finally reached its climax. And everyone was laughing so hard that the tears were streaming down our cheeks. A whole group of McKinney Club Lake regulars were over to our lake house to eat Dad's old-fashioned country breakfast. The night before I had come up to the lake with my girls for a visit with Mom and Dad.

About midnight, Dad awoke me on the sleeping porch and said, "Get up and come over to the island with me to get some tomatoes."

I rolled over and pulled on my clothes and off we walked, flashlights in hand down to the boat dock. Luckily, our eyes adjusted quickly, and the full moon eliminated the need for the flashlight.

As my brain began to sharpen from a dull sleep, I asked, "What in the world are we doing?"

"Shush!" was the only answer I got, as we stepped down into the metal flat-bottom boat that smelled to high heaven from the open container of stink bait. Quickly, Dad pulled the outboard motor on, and off we slid across a dark, still lake. Within a few minutes, we turned into a cove and arrived at a small island. The island was planted with okra, tomatoes, and corn. But our target was the tomatoes!

"Take this bag and fill it up, but only pick the great big tomatoes. Get the biggest ones you can find. I'm going to drive Jim Craig crazy!" Dad snickered, clearly as pleased as any Tom Sawyer.

"What are we doing?" I was still confused. "Why are we out here this time of night, and why are we picking Jim's tomatoes? You have hundreds of tomatoes on the kitchen counter now and more than that in your own garden."

Dad giggled. He clearly was relishing his chance to let me in on the gag on his good friend Jim. "Sissy, you know Jim Craig is a multimillionaire, but he never hit a lick at gardening. He's by nature a really competitive guy, so I'm always pushing and egging him on. Most of us up here at the lake plant a little garden, and every year everyone brags on my tomatoes. Jim just got tired of being left out. So he decided to build the biggest, baddest vegetable garden we had ever seen. And he started shooting off his mouth. He's been bragging down at his place to Al and some of the others about how he was going to show up my tomatoes! He hired himself a highfalutin consultant with some kind of special manure concoction."

"Well, I told all the guys to keep it quiet, and we'd teach old Jim one or two country boy lessons. I've been ragging on him pretty good. I've been telling him that his newfangled manure and corporate experts would have to get up pretty early to beat this old farm boy! For weeks now I've been slipping over to his island garden and pulling his biggest tomatoes and putting them on my counter. It's driving him crazy! He can't figure out why my tomatoes are all so much bigger than his. Tomorrow, when everyone comes over for breakfast, I'm going to let the cat out of the bag. But before I do it, I've got to get the last of the big ones. We are all going to really razz him tomorrow morning before we fess up." At this we both giggled and started to pick furiously.

I was horrified that we were stealing, but at the same time I was tickled at the practical joke that was about to go down. This one was going to be good!

I could see Dad's retort of "you're sure smarter than you look" coming. This expression was another favorite tease. Dad used it often as a fun-loving compliment that let you know he was comfortable enough in the relationship to push your buttons. Beneath his questionable praise was the idea that life should always be fun.

Under the cover of night, we completed our stealth operation and headed back to the shore. As we scurried up the road from the dock, we giggled and speculated about Jim Craig's face when he entered for breakfast only to see a counter loaded with the largest tomatoes anyone had ever seen. How could he possibly believe he could top such a show of strength? Jim would have to acknowledge that Sam Potter was the champ.

The next morning we were up bright and early. All the old standbys would be there. No one ever missed one of Dad's beer biscuit and quail breakfasts. Smothered quail would be great with fresh-picked homegrown tomatoes.

Everyone except Jim was there early. It was "T-day," tomato day. All the grown-up men were snickering like a bunch of naughty little boys.

When Jim arrived, I watched as Dad observed out of the corner of his eye Jim's clear reaction to the tomato-laden counter. Dad came over and handed him a cup of coffee.

"It's been a great year for tomatoes, hasn't it, Jim?" Dad began his setup.

"Yep, it has," Jim mumbled.

"When do you want to pay up on our bet? I haven't seen any tomatoes from you any bigger than mine. Don't you guys think it's time for Jim to put up or shut up?"

Dad was in his element, beaming. As rehearsed, all the guys rallied behind Dad and began to razz Jim.

Al started, "Yep, Jim, you might as well throw in the towel. None of your tomatoes are going to best Sam's. You might as well pay him his twenty. He's got you beat, unless you can pull a tomato the size of a pumpkin out of your pocket."

"Ah, Hell!" Jim stormed, red faced. "I don't know how you did it you son of a gun. I'd have sworn that I had you beat. I don't understand why your tomatoes are so bloody much bigger than mine. I'm going to fire me a horticulturist."

As Dad took Jim's twenty and began to slip it into his pocket, he said, "I wouldn't be too quick about that firing if I were you. That high-priced horticulturist is pretty good after all. Most of the big tomatoes are yours anyway!" And everyone burst into laughter.

"You old son of a gun! You've been stealing my tomatoes!" Jim Craig bellowed as he broke up in laughter.

Dad's quick retort was, "You're sure smarter than you look."

FUN: Joy is where you find it, and if you can't find fun in the day, make some. Age does not have to rob anyone of childhood playfulness or energy for living.

Old age is far more than white hair, wrinkles,
the feeling that it is too late and the game finished,
that the stage belongs to rising generations.
The true evil is not the weakening of the body,
but the indifference of the soul.

–André Maurois

You Can't Teach an Old Dog New Tricks

Flexibility

"Give me your paw," I said for the twentieth time. "Nah, nah, Twisty. Give me your paw, like this." I picked up his paw and gently shook it up and down.

Twisty was our new puppy, a small, screw-tail, black-and-white bulldog. I could see the puzzlement in his eyes as I repeated this exercise over and over. I knew Twisty was smart, so I just kept trying over and over. After hours of patient work and uttering, "Give me your paw," I could finally see Twisty barely move his paw. I squealed with joy and gave him a treat. I knew now it was just a matter of time before Twisty fully understood what I wanted him to do. By the end of the week, Twisty would sit down and hand me his left paw to shake on command. I was so excited. I couldn't wait for Dad to come home for the weekend to see Twisty's new trick.

As soon as Dad arrived, I dragged him straight to the backyard to see Twisty's new trick. Dad was surprised and delighted to see the excitement that the successful training had created in our household.

Dad leaned down and said, "Twisty, give me your paw."

Nothing. Nothing happened at all. Twisty just stared back with his little head tilted in confusion.

Dad just laughed and said, "You do it. He doesn't know what to make of me. Clearly, you have a knack for this sort of thing. You show me."

Sure enough, I asked Twisty to give me his paw, and immediately he lifted his left paw for our practiced shake. "Isn't he smart, Daddy?" I giggled in delight.

"I think you are the smart one, and Twisty is just plain lucky to have you and Sammy Junior to teach him. It's a good thing he's just a pup, 'cause it's hard to teach an old dog new tricks. Let's go eat now. I'm starved."

After dinner, I followed Dad into the TV room. I was thinking about what he said, and I became curious. I wanted to ask Dad some questions.

"Why is it hard to teach an old dog new tricks?" I picked up where Dad left off.

"Well, Sissy, a young puppy is frisky and full of fun and energy. An old dog becomes lazy, sleepy, and lethargic." Dad paused. "Old dogs just don't have the same energy to learn or please their master."

"You know, Suzie Q, people aren't that different from dogs. When we are young, we're full of vinegar, curious, and energetic. We ask questions like your "Why?" As we get older, our energy drops and we grow weary and get very set in our ways. We become too old and entrenched to change." He smiled at me and continued, "In the working world, you've got to keep asking yourself if you've become an old dog. If life is changing and you aren't, then the boss is liable to look for a friskier young pup that is eager to learn. In a way, that's where young people have the advantage over old dogs. If you are smart, you'll learn to think and act like a young dog all your life. No matter how old you become, always be willing to adapt. Sissy, things are always changing."

I walked away wondering, "Could it be that old dogs do not learn new tricks because they do not believe there are any new tricks worth learning?"

Dad did not mean anything deep or profound when he would let us kids know that someone was an "old dog" and unwilling to adapt or change. It was just an assessment that time and age frequently breed inflexibility and an unwillingness to learn and adapt. I am certain when Dad was making these simple pronouncements several decades back, that being an "old dog" was not as economically reckless as it is today.

As parents, we should coach our children that change is constantly taking place. If we stay the same tomorrow as we are today, at some point our skills will be out of date. If we cling to yesterday's learning, we will be labeled old dogs that cannot learn new tricks.

Technology continues to prove that the status quo is certainly not the only way. We live in a rapidly changing society. To survive, we must look ahead and anticipate and explore the way life is changing, could be changed, or should be changed. Change cannot be stopped or slowed.

FLEXIBILITY: Be careful not to get too set in your ways. Life is changing more rapidly than ever, and if we don't change with it, we become outmoded. (Read: *Who Moved My Cheese?* by Stanley Johnson.)

What we call failure
is not the falling down,
but the staying down.

–Mary Pickford

If at First You Don't Succeed, Try, Try Again

Success

"**D**addy, stop him!" I shouted. "He's going to break all of them. Stop it!" I screamed at the top of my lungs.

"What in the world is going on?" Dad said, finally paying attention to my plea.

"Sammy Junior threw all my pick-up-sticks, and he is going to break them," I quickly tattled.

"Well, why did you do that, Sam Junior?" Dad was trying to stop an escalating fight between siblings on Christmas Day. I had gotten a cylinder of long, thin, multicolored pick-up-sticks from Santa. Pick-up-sticks was a game of skill and dexterity, and I couldn't wait to play it. I was too young to understand the competitive advantage I had over my little brother.

In order to play my new game, I convinced Sammy Junior to play with me. What I did not anticipate was the degree of frustration he would experience as I repeatedly trounced him. My age and dexterity created a strong advantage for me. Finally, fed up in frustration,

Sammy Junior picked up my sticks and began throwing them all over the room.

Sammy Junior mumbled, "I don't know, Dad. I don't like this stupid game 'cause I can't do it! She beats me every time."

"Sammy Junior, you've got to *learn* to beat your sister. Trust me, it won't take you that long. She's bigger than you, so she has had more years to get ready for this game. But if you keep playing, you'll get better every time you play. Pretty soon she'll be hollering that she's tired of you beating her. You've got to remember that 99 percent of all things in life are skills, and it just takes repeat practice to get good at any skill. It is like the old proverb: 'If at first you don't succeed, try, try again.'"

"Now, Sissy," Dad continued. "You need to help your brother by trying to coach him a little bit until he learns the game. It is always easier to succeed if you have a coach showing you how. Now, you kids either do it right or we'll have to put away the pick-up-sticks for a while."

"We'll be good, Dad," I quickly added, because I didn't want to lose my new pick-up-sticks.

As Sammy Junior and I grew up, Dad would frequently dust off this old proverb to goad us into patience and to encourage a repeat effort. Even as children, we came to dread this over-used adage. It got to the point that all Mom or Dad had to say was the first few words. By the time either one of them got out the "If at first you don't succeed . . ." Sammy and I were already droning in "we know, try, try again."

Repetition reduces the impact and relevance of anything. The overuse of this adage affected not only Sammy Junior and me; it seems to have had the same impact on most adults. This proverb sounds corny and out of date. But like it or not, this overworked phrase is true. The only way to any level of success is the process of trial and error. There is a recipe for success. The recipe is to start the repetitive process of effort, followed by failure, adjust the process and repeat until you succeed. This is the process of learning anything new. To grow and accomplish, we must continue to try things we do not know how to do. Success is the result of learning from mistakes. The bigger the failure we are willing to experience, the bigger the possible success.

Dad's "If at first you don't succeed, try, try again," were words of encouragement. Our cultural dilemma is that we have spent decades teaching generations of our society that failure is not only bad, but it is shameful.

As young children, we are not afraid of failure. Trial and error is the way we learn to crawl, walk, talk, feed ourselves, read, and write. Virtually everything we achieve is achieved because of our strong willingness to repeatedly try despite failure.

Failure should be encouraged, if we tried and failed and learned something in the process. If we learned, it really was not failure, was it? It was learning.

Children do not have a problem with this concept. They seem to understand that it is just the way things get done. Adults have the problem. Perhaps it is because, unlike children, adults go long periods without trying new things. Perhaps we spend too much time in the safe and easy place of doing what we know. The unwillingness to fail becomes an unwillingness to succeed.

SUCCESS: It is okay to fail your way to success. The majority who create success did it just that way. Give yourself the time with renewed effort to get where you want to go.

As I have said before,
businessmen are no exceptions to the rule
that everyone makes mistakes.

–J. Paul Getty

You're Going To Make Some Mistakes

Failure

*B*y the time I reached the halfway point home from Rosemont Elementary, the tears were streaming down my cheeks. Several blocks later the tears were completely unstoppable. As I ran in the front door, I quickly headed for my bedroom upstairs. It was too late; Mom had seen my red face, and I could hear her voice.

"Suzanne, what is the matter with you? Are you all right?"

"No, I'm not all right." I reached in my notebook and pulled out a paper with a "60" on it. It was my arithmetic paper, and Miss Knox said that Mom and Dad had to sign it.

"I made a horrible grade on my arithmetic test," I sobbed.

"Well, crying about it won't make it any better. You can do better next time."

I wonder what my life choices might have been like if Mom and Dad had not preprogrammed my brain with the belief that mistakes were okay, and that it was never too late to alter the course of events. "You're going to make some mistakes" was a phrase I heard often enough that it helped me overcome the fear of condemnation. Condemnation is the real fear behind the fear of failure.

Failure has finality to it. Too often it becomes a label. The real risk of failure is not the failure itself; it is the potential to permanently label ourselves a failure. Failure is an assessment not an identity. It is an assessment at a given point in time as to whether or not an objective has been met. It is nothing more or less.

Mentally, we give failure more status than it is due. We fantasize about failure being on our record. Our fear of the dreaded failure begins to teach risk avoidance. It sets a pattern for us to under-challenge our capacity. A learning system that rewards under-achievement and encourages students to reach only for what is well within their grasp condemns our intellectual growth as a society. Until we alter our schools to reward effort and allow whatever pace is needed to complete the required work, we will teach fear of failure.

It is very difficult to learn or grow without making mistakes or having an occasional failure. Trial and error is the natural path of learning. If we are afraid of failure, we will not grow our incomes or our society. Mom and Dad gave me permission to explore, to learn, to grow, and to make mistakes. I hope your mom and dad did the same.

FAILURE: Failure is not an identity, so don't claim it as yours. Mistakes are a part of life and a necessary component of learning.

I'm frightened of eggs;
worse than frightened, they revolt me.
That white round thing without any holes . . .
have you ever seen anything more revolting than an
egg yolk breaking and spilling its yellow liquid?
Blood is jolly red. But egg yolk is yellow revolting.
I've never tasted it.
—Alfred Hitchcock

How Do You Like Your Eggs?
. . . Just Fine!

Results

*I*t was summer and Dalton and Mary Ann Gressett with their five children had come for a visit from Oregon. Dalton was my mom's half brother. The Gressett children consisted of four boys and a baby girl. The four boys were little stair-steps led by Eddie, the twins—Ronnie and Sammy—and Stephen; the baby was named Judy. Sammy, one of the Gressett twins, had been named for my Dad. The whole Gressett family, along with Mom, Dad, my brother and myself, were headed to our three-room lake house for a weekend of family fun.

Fun was defined as fishing, playing cards, cooking, eating, and laughing in general. In the evenings, everyone would sleep on the big sleeping porch. Dalton was Mom's favorite half brother. He was a warm and loving man. The Gressett children all called my dad Uncle Sam.

As evening approached that first day, Dad asked Mary Ann what her kids liked for breakfast. Dad's excess weight testified to the fact that he "loved his groceries." Dad's second favorite thing in life was fixing food. Dad planned to get up early the next morning and slip into the main room to cook breakfast.

The main room in the lake house was an all-purpose central room. It had an open, L-shaped family room with a fireplace and an open kitchen. A large, L-shaped eating bar defined the kitchen. Dad had high hopes of starting an early morning country breakfast for eleven hungry lake visitors. So when Dad asked Mary Ann, "What do the kids like for breakfast?" Mary Ann's response to his query was that the boys were very picky eaters. Each boy liked something different, and eggs were not part of that picture. Mary Ann suggested that Dad not cook anything, and she would try to get something simple together for the boys, perhaps Froot Loops.

Dad was having none of this! Half of his fun at a lake visit was the cooking and sharing of a big breakfast. It was his belief that the more limited eating choices were encouraged, the more limited the choices became. With his usual charm, Dad told Mary Ann not to worry about the boys, and he "would handle it." And handle it he did, in typical, fun-loving fashion.

As morning came, I could smell and hear the fresh, hot coffee perking. It engaged all the senses. I did not like coffee as a child, but the coffee smell and the early morning air evoked an intense appetite. As I wandered into the kitchen, I saw on the stove a big cookie sheet of thick, fluffy biscuits, an iron skillet bubbling to the brim with hot cream gravy, a paper plate lined with paper towels loaded four or five inches high with fried bacon and fresh sausage patties. Next to the skillet of gravy was a second skillet filled with scrambled eggs. On the long counter top were fresh, sliced homegrown tomatoes from Dad's garden and, always, a few hot jalapeño peppers. I noticed that all the boys were up and dressed.

I was the oldest of all the children on the outing, and I was the last of the kids to get up to eat. Mom, Mary Ann, and Dalton slept in. Dad was clearly in good humor. With a big grin he told me, "Wait till Mary Ann finds out that the boys ate all their breakfast and cleaned their plates, eggs and all!" Dad was clearly pleased with himself. He told me that Mary Ann was convinced the night before that there was no way her boys would eat eggs for breakfast. Yet, all four boys and my brother ate a huge, farm-style breakfast, scrambled eggs included!

I remember Dad's smile as he bragged about how he got the boys to eat their eggs and love them. Dad's salesmanship did not fail him when he went to work on the kids. The Gressett boys never stood a chance. They were going to eat a Sam Potter breakfast and enjoy doing it. They would leave the breakfast table full and fortified for the day and never know they had been "sold."

Like most young kids, the boys were up at the crack of dawn that morning ready to start the day, but they were not up before Dad. He was way ahead of them in the cooking cycle. As the smell of food stimulated their hungry stomachs, Dad gave the boys their marching orders. Typical of Dad's approach to life, he made eating breakfast a fun game. This time it was military style. He told the boys to play hard until breakfast was ready, and as soon as it was done, he would call them to come eat immediately.

They were instructed to line up according to age. The oldest, Eddie, was to go first and be in charge of leading the way. Each boy was to pick up a paper plate, silverware and a napkin, and "report" to the stove in a "military line, ready for duty." Dad told them when he called their name out, they were to step up to the stove "at attention," hold out their plate and he would help it. Dad instructed them to extend their plates, arms fully straightened in front, and when he asked them; "How do like your eggs, boys?" they were to say, "Just fine, Uncle Sam, I like them just fine."

The humor and fun of the game was not lost on the boys. They were intrigued by the exciting new game. The young Gressett squad ate a hearty breakfast that morning, and everyone cleaned his plate.

It was easy to see why old and young alike loved my dad. He approached everything as play.

When Mary Ann awoke, Dad could not wait to tell her how all the boys finished their eggs without a peep.

Every day of the lake visit we all lined up, paper plates in hand, and no matter what kind of eggs were served, when Daddy asked, "How do you like your eggs?" we all laughed, kids and grown-ups alike, and said, "Just fine, Uncle Sam, we like them just fine!"

RESULTS: Beliefs, opinions, and results can be altered with the right approach to the problem. Change the input and you change the output. Sometimes, we need to change our strategy and approach a situation from a new perspective.

No person was ever honored
for what he received.
Honor has been the reward
for what he gave.
—Calvin Coolidge

You Can Dish It Out,
But You Can't Take It

Give and Take

$\mathcal{A}$s Dad scooped up his winnings, he slapped the
floor and proclaimed, "I'm the champ and you're the chump." As
Sammy Junior began to groan, Dad chimed in with his usual attitude
coaching, "You can dish it out, but you can't take it." Life was fun!
Find the fun or make the fun yourself, it didn't matter which.

Playing cards was a favorite way to while away a lazy summer weekend at the family lake house. The sophistication of the card
game was determined by the age of the youngest child present. The
game was selected to include *everyone.* So it was a time to play
"War," "Go Fish," "Gin Rummy," "Poker," or "High, Low, Jick, Jack,
and the Game" as the maturity level dictated.

I remember that day, sitting in a circle on the hardwood floor
of the McKinney Club Lake clubhouse playing a game of poker.
There was Dad, myself, Sammy Junior, a little boy about seven, J. J.
Lemmon, and several crusty old fishermen all playing cards and
laughing together. Everyone sat on the floor like a bunch of kids, only

the "kids" were ages six to mid-fifties. We were being taught poker while betting the high stakes of toothpicks or matchsticks to test our luck and hilarious lack of skill against one another.

Many years later, I found Dad at it again. Not with Sammy Junior and myself, but with his granddaughters, each taking her turn to bond and laugh with her grandfather, "Honey."

When Dad won a game, he always had some humorous remark. "You can dish it out; but you can't take it" was one of many. Other times it was "I'm the champ and you're the chump." Dad's crazy sayings made the games fun. They also served as a subtle lesson that the losers in any game had no right to spoil the fun with bad humor or hostile dispositions, both forbidden in the Potter household. Nothing was worse than a sore loser. We learned at a young age that if you played, you would lose as well as win. Dad's attitude made it clear that if you only had fun when you won, you were going to be miserable most of the time. He never told us that the philosophy he applied to card games applied to life as well. Some life lessons are just assumed.

GIVE AND TAKE: Life isn't a zero-sum game. If you want to have a good time, you have to be willing to give a good time. We must look for our own joy, even when we feel others are beating us in the competitive game of life.

Courage is being scared to death—
and saddling up anyway.

–John Wayne

You Can Run, but You Cannot Hide

Accountability

$\mathcal{A}$s I came in the back door with groceries from the country store, I could hear my daughter Nikki's voice so loud that it was approaching a shout. "High, low, jick, jack and the game!" she was yelling out, followed by a chorus from Dad, "I can run, but I cannot hide! You're killing us little girl!"

Translation: my eight-year-old daughter was creaming Dad and her two sisters in a card game lovingly known as "High, Low, Jick, Jack and the Game." Nikki was only duplicating her grandfather's behavior when he had a good hand. When Dad won and made his bid, he was going to brag about it! And if you won, he was going to brag on you!

Over the years of growing up, all my girls had their day of winning at cards. They loved to play with Dad because of his outrageous exhibitionism. If Dad was sure he had a winning hand, he would start the theatrics early on. He would tease his opponents as he began a clean sweep by warning, "Girls, you can run, but you cannot hide." And sure enough, before you knew what hit you, he was announcing his win with a shout, "High, low, jick, jack and the game!"

What is interesting about his good-time teasing was the duality of its message. The words themselves tell very real tales of responsibility. How many times would we all like to run away and hide from the harsh realities that we face? There have been times in my life when I have wished I could run. At those times, I recall Dad's words of wisdom: "You can run, but you cannot hide."

I have to laugh at the outrageous notion that a warning from a card game has become life instructive, but wisdom is like that. Wisdom sometimes comes from strange places. If we will listen, we will learn.

Dad's words became deeply lodged in my brain. I was taught during those card games to believe that hiding is not possible, and running only delays the inevitable. Because of his simple instruction through this playful boast, I have been much more ready to take ownership of things that I would rather not.

ACCOUNTABILITY: You cannot run from the cards life deals you. Take ownership of what you have been dealt and play the best game you can. You can't change the hand, but you can change how you play it.

Life is like a round of golf.
When you get out of one hole,
you head for another.

–Brendan Gardner

If It Wasn't for Bad Luck,
I'd Have No Luck at All

Humor

*I*t was as hot a summer as I had ever known in Port Aransas. But as always, we were having a great time on our annual summer vacation. This July was especially fun because Hazel and A. C. Dunn had come to the Gulf Coast with us. The more people, the more fun. That was the way it always was with Mom and Dad. To make this vacation even more fun, A. C. had never been fishing, much less deep-sea fishing, and Dad was determined to broaden A. C.'s horizons.

We spent the first few days walking the beach, crabbing, and eating all the fresh seafood we could hold. On the fourth day, we got up at 4:30 A.M. and headed down to the wharf to the small, leased fishing boats. Dad, A. C., and I were going to take a small charter boat way out from the safety of shore and do some deep-sea fishing. Even though I was only nine, I had been deep-sea fishing once before, and I was really looking forward to the trip.

An hour out into the Gulf, our captain stopped the engine and set each of us up with our fishing gear. We were fishing for kingfish. A kingfish was a medium-sized sport fish that was abundant in Gulf waters. The likelihood of having a fun-filled day catching fish was high. As we put all three lines out into the water and started to troll, Dad had a strike. It was so exciting. I could see A. C. was flustered by Dad's instantaneous success. After all, he wasn't too sure what to do, and there had been no time for coaching. As Dad was fighting his fish and reeling it closer to the boat, A. C. got a strike on his line. I started to reel my line in, but it was too late. Another fish hit my line. I managed to get my fish close to the boat first. Then A. C. lost his fish. Dad's fish was coming in on the left side of the boat, and mine was over on the right. Billy, the captain, quickly grabbed my line to hold my fish steady, and he handed A. C. the big gaff hook. Billy told A. C. to hook Dad's fish and pull it in. Big mistake. A. C. was as nervous as a first-time midwife. He leaned way out over the side and swung at the fish with the gaff. The fish jumped out of the water and startled A. C. so badly that he dropped the gaff overboard and lost the fish off Dad's hook. The gaff was quickly carried off on the high cresting waves. We still had my fish on the hook and no gaff.

A. C. lost the only gaff hook. But instead of being angry, Dad just started laughing. Dad said, "A. C., if you don't want me to show you up by catching the most fish, you could at least just say so! There was no need to throw the only gaff hook on board away just to get rid of my fish. Rather than have poor Billy lose his gaff, I'd have just not taken a pole." A. C. was starting to laugh with all this razzing and told my dad that he was a "no good son of a gun." Dad popped a cold canned Coke and smiled as he said, "You know you're not going to live long enough to live this one down." Jokes continued to come forth as we tried to figure out how to land my fish.

We found a large old hook on board and a length of rope.

Billy threaded the eye of the hook with the rope to create a substitute gaff. About that time Billy spotted a big ling fish that had just moved up into the shade of our boat. It was bigger than any fish I had ever seen, and it was so close to the boat you could almost touch it. The ling fish wouldn't take anything but live bait, so Billy quickly found a live shrimp, put it on a new reel, and told Dad to try to get the ling to take the bait. It wasn't too long before Dad had a huge ling on the hook up next to the boat. Billy was still trying to hold my kingfish to the other side to give Dad room to maneuver. Billy laughed and told A. C. and me that we were going to have to figure out how to gaff that fish with a loose rope hook.

The problem was that the original gaff hook was at the base of a long wooden pole that gave it hooking leverage when a fish was brought alongside the boat. Without the stiff wooden pole, hooking the fish with a rope gaff became a very interesting problem. The new gaff had no support. It was without leverage. A. C., Dad, and I must have looked like the Three Stooges fishing, as we extended our upper bodies out over the side of the boat, diligently working to get the gaff into our catch. The fish knew he had the upper hand! He jumped and splashed and made certain that we paid the price for bringing him on board. The biggest catch of the morning leapt high in the water alongside the boat and came down with a tremendous splat. Water flew into the air, covering us and filling the floor of the boat. Dad wiped the salt water from his glasses, and laughing, said, "Hey A. C., this is a pretty big price to pay just to beat me out of a fishing bet!"

Hours later, we were soaking wet, our hair was sticky with salt, and our shoes squeaked. It took most of the morning and early afternoon but finally we landed the ling. We had laughed so hard at our miserable attempts to outwit the fish that we were worn-out. But we were happy.

That fishing trip was one of the most fun-filled days of my life. If the events had gone smoothly, the day would have been fun. As it was, disaster handled with humor made the day both memorable and joyous. I loved A. C. for being there and Dad for just being Dad.

I was a grown woman before I knew that there were people who viewed life very differently. It never occurred to me that other people might have taken the unforeseen mishaps in an angry way and been mad that their fishing trip was spoiled. Intolerance and inflexibility rob life of its inherent joy and destroy potential pleasure for everyone. Attitudes and perceptions are like germs—they infect everyone nearby.

As we returned to the beach cottage, Hazel and Mom asked if we had any luck. We all did a double take, looked at each other and burst into laughter, as Dad with familiar wit said, "If it wasn't for bad luck, we'd have no luck at all."

Dad's saying, "If it wasn't for bad luck, I'd have no luck at all," became more than a funny phrase for me. Through the years, I learned that I could change my attitude by using this tool of ironic humor. In life, events large and small move in ways that we wish had not occurred. If we acknowledge the unexpected and move forward and find humor in the moment, we defuse the stresses in life. We all face dark periods where we know that, "If it wasn't for bad luck, we'd have no luck at all."

HUMOR: Life delivers the unexpected. Our attitude determines how we experience it. Cultivate an attitude that creates fun and pleasure out of "bad luck."

The reason they fail?
Actually, it's all in the mind.
Like it or not, there is a thing that can
be called The Millionaire Mentality.

–J. Paul Getty

How We Survive and Thrive:
Money

Money Won't Make You Happy

Happiness

I was back in Dallas for a summer visit with Mom
and Dad. It was so good to be home. We had moved to Fort Wayne,
Indiana, and the winter had been rough. I missed the Texas sunshine
the most. Mom took my three girls, Kristy, Suzy, and Nikki to the grocery store, while I unpacked and talked to Dad.

"Mom said you have been traveling a lot with Jim Craig in his
private jet. She said something about the fact that he offered you a
job. What's that about?" I wanted to find out from Dad what kind of
job Jim had asked him to do. Dad had been retired for several years,
and a few years back he met Mr. Craig through one of his neighbors.

Dad and Jim hit it off immediately. Jim was a self-made multimillionaire and loved horses. Jim was raising racehorses as a hobby,
and he was flying all over the U.S. to race. Dad said that Jim was a
very competitive person, and he loved the thrill of competing with his
horses. I knew Mom and Dad went with the Craigs to the Kentucky

Derby, but beyond that I thought it was just a fun friendship. I couldn't imagine Dad wanting to give up his retirement lifestyle.

"Oh, Suzie, your mom is making too much out of this. Jim wanted to put me on his payroll as a consultant. I told him 'No.' I've given him advice from time to time, just man-to-man talking about how to handle different investments and employee issues and such. Well, I guess he found a lot of benefit in my suggestions, and he wanted to hire me and put me on payroll as an advisor."

"So, it wouldn't be a regular job? That might be fun then," was my response.

"Nope, the money he offered is a lot for what I would be willing to do, and I don't want to change our relationship. I don't want to feel that I'm not giving full value, and I don't want Jim to think he's paying for more than he's getting. I don't need the money for your mom and me to be okay, so I won't do it. I don't need big fancy planes and cars to make me happy. I'm happy with things just the way they are. I told Jim he could have any advice I've got to give for free. We're friends and that is enough."

"Daddy, that makes sense to me. Whatever makes you happy makes me happy. But it was flattering."

"Suzie, sometimes I wonder if Jim really understands where I am coming from." Dad's eyes seemed to sparkle with humor as he spoke.

"What do you mean, Daddy?"

"So many people think you have to be making money to be happy. Money won't make you happy! It never has and it never will. Not having enough can sure make you miserable, but happiness comes from somewhere else. It comes, in large part, from being satisfied with your life and appreciative of the opportunities you've been given. I've known a lot of people that were rich in dollars and still miserable. It doesn't take that much to make me happy. I don't need a brand-new car or alligator shoes to have a good time."

I leaned over and gave him a kiss and said, "I love you, Daddy."

It is true that some of the most useful life lessons Dad taught me were about money. Dad was very money savvy. He knew a lot about the principles of money management, and he made a conscious effort to let Sammy Junior and me know that there were some key principles that we should learn. Dad emphasized the lessons about money so often that it would be easy to misconstrue his advice as being money driven. To conclude that would be to miss completely the other lessons Daddy taught me.

This section of my book on surviving and thriving is heavily focused on Dad's teachings on money, but there is more here than that. It is important to note that Dad never believed money was the source of happiness. He often pointed out that happiness was a choice. I never heard him say that happiness was a choice available only to those with money.

Dad was quick to point out that people who were often miserable did not lack financially. That is precisely why I placed this often-used phrase of Dad's at the beginning of this section analyzing our relationship to money.

Far too many Americans seek money as the answer to happiness. "Money won't make you happy." It just makes one of life's problems go away.

Dad knew that happiness was found or lost in our attitude. Money is a medium of exchange and a necessary tool in modern society. Dad's money lessons are about financial survival and well-being. Lack of money can make life very difficult. Because Dad understood firsthand the difficulty that a lack of money can create, he was determined that my brother and I would understand the importance of handling money properly.

The Potters were just your average, middle-class, American family. That is how I was brought up. I was a very happy child, but it was Dad and Mom's love of life that made me happy, nothing more. I would trade all the money in the world for one more happy day with my mom and dad.

HAPPINESS: Happiness is an emotional feeling produced by your attitude toward life. Money is a medium of exchange, a thing, not a feeling. Money cannot of itself make you happy or unhappy.

What I know about money,
I learned the hard way—by having it.

–Margaret Halsey

Saving for a Rainy Day

Insurance

"*W*hat are you doing, Sissy? Saving for a rainy day?"
Dad had just walked into my bedroom to find me on my knees
with all my dollar bills and pennies and nickels spread out on the bed.

Sammy Junior and I started getting an allowance from Mom
and Dad when I was about eight. We were each paid a one-dollar bill
for doing some assigned weekly chores. We could do anything we
wanted with our wages. It was our money to spend, to save, or to do
anything we chose to do. Earning money and learning how to handle
it was an important lesson in the Potter household.

I had a fascination with the whole allowance process. It was
my first step into the adult world of independence. It was the first
time I can remember being given full control of an asset of any kind.
Up until I had an allowance, others controlled everything in my
young world. I went to bed when I was told. I took a bath when I was
told. I ate dinner when I was called. But the dollar, my allowance,
was mine to control.

I wasn't really sure what to do with the money, but I thought about all the things Dad had told me about spending and saving. I had heard him say to Mom that they had to save for a rainy day. I overheard him kidding with Fred Lorenz, a longtime friend, that he would rather "make interest than pay it."

When you are six, making interest and saving for a rainy day does not have much meaning. Nonetheless, things your parents say stick in your mind.

I saved my pennies and nickels, and I wrapped my dollar bills around an adhesive tape dispenser that I kept hidden in my sock drawer. Even at the age of six, my dad had aroused my interest in saving money. Dad had begun to transfer his beliefs to me.

As I experimented with saving money, I became more intrigued. The options that unfolded as I saved more and more began to expand my thinking. While this was only a mind game in the head of a very young child, the seeds of understanding were beginning to sprout. I knew that the more money I had, the more choices I had.

When I had only a nickel left from spending my allowance, I knew there were very few things that could be bought for a nickel. I realized that when I had saved up five weeks of allowance, or five dollars, there were dozens of things that my five dollars could buy. Many of the things I wanted cost less than five dollars. Even the left-over change from a purchase still afforded me many more possible purchases. The mental game of thinking about what I would buy was almost as much fun as buying.

My first money experiences did not focus on the rainy day that Dad spoke of. I had no idea what his kind of rainy day was. I also did not have any idea what interest was. Consequently, paying versus earning interest was a lesson that would have to wait until a later date. I did learn about the income and spending cycle. I understood the logic of my first money principle, which was "more money gives you more choices." I never forgot the value of that first childhood conclusion. It has influenced many of my financial decisions. Who would have thought that a one-dollar allowance could have such an impact?

INSURANCE: Money in small amounts has limited uses. The more money you have the more choices you have about its use. We are never too young to start saving for a rainy day. The ultimate life insurance is money.

Can anybody remember
when times were not hard
and money not scarce?

–Ralph Waldo Emerson

A Penny Saved Is a Penny Earned

Benjamin Franklin, *Poor Richard's Almanack*

Saving

*D*ad was pushing his big toe around on top of the sand, and all of a sudden he hollered, "Hey, kids, look what I found."

Sammy Junior and I quickly turned and ran back to see what treasure he had discovered. The surf had gone out as evening approached, and we were scouring the beach for sand dollars. Mom had great eyes, and usually if anyone was going to find a treasure in the surf it would be her, so we were sticking close. But today it was Dad.

As Sammy Junior and I ran toward Dad, he was holding out two gritty, dark brown pennies. "Ugh," we sighed in disappointment.

"What is the matter with you two?" he said. "Don't you know 'a penny saved is a penny earned'? Put them in your pocket, and don't turn your nose up at found money! Ole Ben Franklin was onto something when he said that hundreds of years ago. It was valuable advice then, and it is even more valuable now."

Sammy Junior grabbed his penny and stuck it in the top of his paper cup filled with shells and their gray sandy grit, then he took off to catch up with Mom to look for "real treasure."

I stayed behind with Dad. "Why is Ben Franklin's advice more valuable now, Dad?"

"Taxes," he muttered with a tone of disapproval.

"I don't understand."

"Well," he began to explain, "When Ole Ben said that a penny saved is a penny earned, he was right. But today, a penny you save is *more* important than a penny you earn. When Ben was alive, this country didn't have income tax. Today, when you work, the government takes part of your pay. They get a big piece of your check before you do. So to have a penny or a dollar to save, you have to *earn more* than that penny or dollar. You have to pay Uncle Sam his pound of flesh *before* you can even think about saving. In this country, we call it 'take-home pay.' So anything you save for the future costs you more to earn than the savings itself. You kids need to know that pennies will add up. They are worth more in terms of your earnings than their face value. Don't ever waste money, no matter how small! Hang onto it, and over time it will add up and pay you back for the effort. Money is not an ungrateful friend. You take care of it and get to know it, and in your old age it will take care of you."

SAVING: Understand the difference in the value of pretax and posttax money. Never assume small quantities of money saved over time won't create value. It is faulty thinking. See Appendixes A–E.

Money is better than poverty,
if only for financial reasons.

–Woody Allen

Don't Let Money Burn a Hole
in Your Pocket

Spending

*A*unt Bessie looked down at me with her soft, hazel-gray eyes. To a little girl of five, Aunt Bessie looked very old. Her hair was the color of charcoal, with veins of silver running in every direction. The style was neither glamorous nor fashionable. Perhaps Mom's movie-star looks overshadowed my ability to judge age.

Aunt Bessie was my great aunt on Mom's side. Aunt Bessie and "Pop" Darr lived down at the end of the block on Waco Street. Aunt Bessie had opened a small soda pop and candy store in the front room of her home. I remember looking at all the yummy stuff and Dad saying, "What's the matter, little girl? Is your money burning a hole in your pocket?"

That was the first time, but not the last time, that Dad would ask me that question. Dad didn't wait for an answer. He just laughed as I pulled some money out of a little pink leather purse that I loved to carry. I carefully counted out three pennies and took three matching pieces of bubble gum from a slightly tilted glass jar. As I paid for my gum, Dad grabbed my hand and gave it a gentle squeeze. He knew I had more loose change in my little purse that I was holding for later.

Money that burned a hole in someone's pocket was the way Dad referred to undisciplined spending. He always said it in fun and usually with a laugh, and his clear blue eyes glistened with affection. If I had spent all my change on candy, Dad wouldn't have said a word; but I could tell he was pleased that I had not.

It is odd how you remember certain things. Learning from what is not said is as powerful as learning from what is said. Dad was proud that my brother and I had "a few dimes to rub together." Mom and Dad rarely had treats when they were children. It was a part of Dad's joy to see that we had the wherewithal to burn that hole.

No one had to explain what it meant to have money burn a hole in your pocket. The metaphor was too vivid even for a preschooler to misinterpret. The spender had just lost control of the money. Over the years, I began to understand that Dad did not allow money to burn a hole in his pocket. Daddy chose to stay in control of his money. He did not let money control him. Part of that discipline was driven by the desire to give Mom, Sammy Junior, and me all of the things he never had. He kept his money messages short, sweet, and repetitive because he wanted my brother and me to learn how to accumulate and manage money.

SPENDING: Don't let today's desires cloud the vision for tomorrow's needs. Restraint in spending needs to start young. Reward the maturity of the frugal child. The discipline to save must be encouraged and developed. Without asset accumulation, there is no possibility for retirement or funds for emergencies. See Appendix E.

Money Doesn't Grow on Trees

Respect

*S*ammy Junior was running so fast that his light brown hair was flying back off his forehead and standing up in the air. Mom, Dad, and I had just opened the front door to the McKinney Club Lake House. Sammy Junior and our cousin, Georgie, spotted us right away.

"Daddy, Daddy, give Georgie and me some more nickels right away. Come look at this great machine."

J. J. Lemmon, who owned the private lake, had bought three old nickel slot machines. Sammy Junior and Georgie found them. They had used up all their own nickels and wanted more.

Dad just laughed, dug deep into his pocket and pulled out a fistful of change. He pulled out all the nickels and handed them to Sammy Junior and said, "Now share those with Georgie and your sister." I ran after them to see what they were so excited about.

What fun we had! We must have had seven or eight nickels apiece. As we put them in, the machine rolled round and round, with all the exciting metallic reels spinning in a blur of color. Then Sammy Junior hit a small jackpot. We all squealed and jumped up and down, splitting the winnings and hitting the machines again.

I could hear Dad across the room, laughing at our fun. Predictably, we were soon out of nickels and we were running back for more.

"Daddy, Daddy, please . . . pretty please, can we have some more nickels?"

"What do you kids think? Do you think that money grows on trees?" he said.

We knew that Dad had a bunch of quarters. We saw them in the handful of change he pulled out earlier, so . . . "Please, Daddy, please . . . pretty please, with sugar on it?" we all begged.

Dad laughed good-naturedly as always and went over to J. J. Lemmon and asked for three dollar's worth of nickels. Dad bent down slowly to where his eyes were directly across from ours and in quiet measured tones said, "Now, guys, this is *your* money. You can save it. Buy candy with it. Give it away. Go to the movies. Or gamble it all away . . . just for the fun of it. Make sure you like what you are doing with *your* money, because when it is gone, there isn't going to be any more. Figure out how much you're willing to lose *before* you start to play and stick to it.

He smiled a big grin, but it was clear by his tone that he was very serious.

Dad gave us each a handful of nickels, and as we raced off to the "one-armed-bandits," I could hear him holler, "Remember, money doesn't grow on trees. You have to earn it and pay taxes to have it."

Dad always seemed to know how to walk the thin line between being an easy touch and a tightwad.

There was no question Mom and Dad loved to indulge Sammy Junior and me, but never at the risk that we would lose our grounding. Too much indulgence and expectations set in. Respect for the labor that it takes to create money was an important life principle. Mom and Dad said that money was a necessary tool, and we need to have respect for it, know what it is to have it, and what it is to be without it.

Off we ran to our new toy.

As the wheels turned, the nickels jingled in the slots. You could hear Dad say, "I'll bet you five of your nickels that you guys lose it faster than I made it." He laughed and turned back around.

RESPECT: Respect for money is a taught attitude just like respect for your elders is a taught attitude. It is our parents' responsibility to teach us both. It is our responsibility to teach our children.

The irony is that for many people
who cling desperately to money,
the money they spend for things of
very little value . . . is why they are poor.

–Robert Kiyosoki

Penny-Wise and Pound-Foolish

Judgment

"*H*op in the car. We're going over to the A & P," Mom announced as she slid her sunglasses back onto her face, loaded the toothpaste and napkins in the backseat of our copper-brown 1949 Pontiac and handed me a chocolate ice cream cone.

It was a very hot Texas summer. The misery of a humid, hundred-plus day needs to be experienced only once for you to know that you don't want to be in a hot car at midday.

"But why Mom? It's hot and I want to go home."

"It won't take much longer, but we need to go to the grocery store."

"Well, why did we drive all the way over to Skillerns to buy this stuff when we needed to go to the A & P, anyway? The A & P has toothpaste and napkins, too!"

"Saving money, little girl. You always need to watch your pennies. Your dad is real smart, and he says that it is important not to pay too much for things."

Mom was just doing her job. She was not only the chief cook

and bottle washer but Mom was also the watchdog of the family budget.

Skillerns was a very nice drug store, but its proximity to our house on Montreal Street was not one of its attributes. Skillerns was a fifteen-minute drive from home. The A & P was at least another ten minutes in the other direction. I was grateful for the chocolate ice cream cone that was rapidly melting in the heat. But even as a chubby child of ten, I couldn't help but silently question the wisdom of all this running around. Sweat began to trickle down my temple as fast as the melting ice cream ran down my cone. All I could think about was that I hoped Mom had saved a lot because I was miserable.

Mom knew how to be "penny-wise." But I never saw her consider the cost of the pursuit. To my knowledge, Mom never examined the *net* savings of an activity. She only looked at the *gross* savings. It never occurred to Mom that it was important to evaluate the cost of gasoline and worn tires, not to mention the ice cream bribe, against the pennies saved on toothpaste and napkins. Perhaps there was a real economic benefit, but I was too hot and too young to care.

As I sat in the backseat licking my drippy cone, I caught my mind focusing on something Dad often uttered, "Penny-wise and pound-foolish." My young brain mentally repeated this phrase the minute Mom said she was watching the "pennies." I wondered, "What is a 'pound' anyway?" I concluded, as I took another quick lick of my cone, that "penny-wise" took a lot of work!

Looking back over my life, I now know, that Mom never understood the big picture of money. Since Dad understood, she did not think she needed to learn. Mom understood only bits and pieces about how to get ahead financially. For her, marriage was a partnership, and it was no more complicated than that. Each partner had a different job, and that was that. The cultural wisdom of my mother's day was for her not to "worry her pretty little head" about such things as money. Truthfully, Mom really didn't want to learn about business. To her, it was boring work.

Mom was a glamorous woman with an artistic spirit. She would much rather shop at a big shoe clearance for another "bargain" pair of shoes or find a great hat. Mom was so focused on saving the pennies, she never learned to master bigger money issues.

When Dad died in 1986, Mom was financially provided for, but she didn't know what to do with what she had. She was lost without my dad, both emotionally and financially.

Mom lived the later years of her life ill-equipped to deal with the financial decisions she needed to make. She was inexperienced and had no time left to learn and recover from her mistakes. All of a sudden, she had to "worry her pretty little head" about it, and she did not know what to do.

JUDGMENT: We know that we must pay attention to our expenses and overhead. We know that we need to save money and cut costs. Yet, most of us don't have the wisdom to do what needs to be done. We are "fools" acting out foolish behavior, when we should know better. We lack the self-discipline to live our lives with good judgment.

'Tis money that begats money.

–English Proverb

Money Is the Only Thing I Know
That Will Work for You
Twenty-Four Hours a Day

Money's Power

*D*ad slapped a silver dollar on the glass top cotton-candy stand at the state fair. "Give me two cotton candies," he said. As Dad handed Sammy Junior and me our cotton candy and reached for his change, he said, "Kids, you see this money? Money is the only thing I know that will work for you twenty-four hours a day. And it can buy some pretty good cotton candy, too!" Dad's idea was that a little bit of sugar makes the learning go down easier. Dad slipped his bits of wisdom into his conversation as editorial comment.

Dad never taught my brother or me how to put money to work twenty-four hours a day. Sammy Junior and I clearly understood doing it had two steps: First, save some money. Second, invest it. I don't think we understood much more than that in the early years of our lives. Since Dad found his own way in life, he believed that we would find our financial way also. Specific advice such as buy bonds or invest in real estate were foolish recommendations because economies change and values shift. Investment advice is both time- and circumstance-sensitive. All Dad could do was to ground us with basic principles and give us the motivation to learn the rest. If we were shown the direction, we could make our own paths.

In Dad's day, the man in the family was the breadwinner, and marriage was a lifetime commitment. I think Dad believed that when I got married my financial security would be taken care of in the same way he had taken care of Mom. The change in the financial responsibilities of women and the financial requirements posed by a longer life expectancy was something Dad did not anticipate.

I was very fortunate to have had those early financial lessons. My husband did not share my dad's philosophy toward conservative spending, and our financial lives played the zero-sum game of spending all we made.

But I knew that Dad's plan worked. He had proved it by the time my second daughter was born. After thirty years as a traveling salesman, Dad retired from Potts-Knaur Leather Company at the ripe old age of fifty-five. I knew from Dad's instruction that the only escape from "the work till you drop" treadmill was to have an alternative method to provide monthly cash flow.

When Dad said, "pay yourself first," he was trying to teach both my brother and me a disciplined method to accumulate savings. Dad believed Sammy Junior and I could figure out, just as he had, how to grow and multiply our "nest egg." From Dad's perspective, starting *early* and saving *every* payday was the most important step for us to learn. If Dad could not teach us this, then nothing else was going to matter anyway.

When Dad said, "Money is the only thing I know that will work for you twenty-four hours a day," he was emphasizing the benefit of accumulating working assets. This saying gave us the reason to pay ourselves first. Money could and would work for us if we would only learn its ways.

As long as we have to trade our lives, measured by time and skill for our wages, then we are forced to live a life of survival and limited choices. On the other hand, if we accumulate money and learn how to make it work for us, then we have bought our freedom.

I look forward to the day when my money will work for me twenty-four hours a day so that I don't have to continue to work for my survival. I have that as a goal, and I have a plan. If you never make financial independence a goal or start to execute a plan, then you will never get there. The only choice left to the undisciplined is a life of limited time and limited resources. Those thoughts alone make a compelling argument for discipline.

MONEY'S POWER: It takes money to survive. You can work till you die, or you can find something or someone else to work for you. If you own investments that can generate as much money as you need for personal survival, then, and only then, have you achieved financial independence. How can you get those investments? It all starts with the commitment to save money specifically for investing.

*. . . but he who gathers money
little by little makes it grow.*

-Proverbs 13:10

I'd Rather Collect Interest than Pay It

Assets Versus Debt

It was Tuesday morning. It was passbook savings day at Rosemont Elementary School. It was my job to remind Mom that it was Tuesday and I needed a dollar for the homeroom savings deposit. Dad told me, "It is important to get in the regular habit of saving money, even if it doesn't seem like a lot at first."

I was taught I had to save "if I ever wanted to have anything." Too young to fully comprehend, I followed parental instructions.

Saving seemed dull at first; however, I was intrigued with the process. I remember watching the account for months. I still remember when the balance hit five dollars. It took me weeks longer than it should have because I would often forget my dollar.

I vaguely remember the teacher posting a few pennies as interest. It was so peculiar to see the round number of the dollars transformed as the pennies were added on a quarterly basis. The small, blue, leather-bound passbook looked odd with a few cents tacked on the end. The whole easy numbers were gone forever.

I felt like my money was going nowhere. Where was this miracle of compound interest that Dad called "the eighth wonder of the world?" I had no sense of excitement, only a feeling of curiosity about the process. Interest posted again. Again it was only a few pennies. I was not impressed with this eighth wonder; it took too long, and it was too slow.

By fifth grade, it began to make sense to me that if I kept the money in the savings account, the interest would earn interest for me right along with the money I put in. I was surprised that someone would pay me another few pennies on the few pennies they had given me earlier. What a neat idea. I was earning money on money that was not mine. I was hooked. Someone besides me was putting money in *my* savings account. It took more than two years, but I was beginning to understand the miracle of compound interest, a geometric form of growth.

I didn't know that the frequency of the compounding could increase the power of this "eighth wonder." I was too young, and I only had the singular experience of a passbook account that compounded quarterly. It wasn't until I took algebra in junior high that I was told that compounding could be annual, semiannual, quarterly, monthly, or even daily. I learned that the frequency of compound interest increases the return. I also began to wonder, "What else do I not know about money that is important?"

I was beginning to understand why Dad told me, to "Learn all you can about everything you can. You can always forget what you don't need, but it is real hard to use what you don't have."

Still, I was not deeply impressed as a young child. The dollars were so small and the process seemed to take forever. As strange and wonderful as the interest compounding seemed, it was still basically a dull and boring process. So my savings just became a habit that I did not want to quit, because it was so easy, and because the other kids were doing it. I did not want to be left out.

School savings was not the only place I began learning about money. At home, I was given an allowance for helping out around the house. It was a dollar a week. I hid it in a roll of old-fashioned adhesive tape that came in a metal container shaped like a flattened donut. The outer cover snapped on and off to keep it totally encased. I would fold the dollar the long way over and over until it was the width of the adhesive tape container. I would then wrap it tightly around and around the center spool. Even as a child, I knew that money must be kept secure. I would occasionally spend a little, but the feeling of having my own private stash thrilled me. It made me feel grown up. I also liked the security that the saved dollars gave me.

I always knew that if I found something I wanted I had some money to buy it. I would fantasize about a hundred different things that my money would let me buy. As long as I had money, I could have any dream my money would buy; or better yet, I was setting goals for saving for some unknown dream item.

Over time, my tape holder became thick and full. The problem was, I would lose count. I couldn't remember how much money I had saved. Occasionally, I would shut myself in my room and quietly take out my adhesive tape dispenser. I would carefully take each rolled dollar off the tape dispenser. I would unfold each one, piling them one on the other in a stack like the cashiers always did. It was great fun. It made me feel rich and important. I would think about all the fun things I could buy all at once. If I bought *this*, I would have enough left over to buy *that*, or maybe I would buy one great big thing all at once.

Sometimes, I thought about how much money I could save if I added more to my passbook savings. But, most of the time, I would save in my secret spot and go on shopping trips where I would spend the money. There were lessons to be learned there also. I learned to shop for value to weigh quality versus price. When I spent my own money, I remembered the lessons longer.

In the summer, I was free to save and spend and spend and save. In the fall, when school would start again, I would be torn between my save and spend cycle and the mysterious passbook account, where someone else was saving with me.

I was irritated on the Tuesday mornings I forgot to ask Mom for the dollar savings deposit. I watched the other kids who were putting in their deposits, and I felt left out and angry with myself for falling behind. I did not feel comforted that most of the other children forgot or did not participate in the savings plan that day. I only compared myself to the ones who did. Even though I was not allowed to spend my passbook savings, I knew I was getting free money from Mom and Dad that was not part of my allowance.

My little passbook savings grew, and I began to think of it as the nest egg Dad always talked about, the nest egg that Dad said everyone should have. I knew this was part of a process that my dad wanted me to learn; he called it "pay yourself first."

It was not a struggle for me to save as a child, because in the beginning my savings account didn't cost me anything. My very first efforts to save were all positive because the money to start was a free gift. Thanks to my parents' support, I had none of the negative emotion that savings has for most people. I did not have to give up other things to start my savings. To save money as adults, we must choose to not spend the money on something that might be pretty, fun, or just plain exciting. Spending always seems exciting and savings always seems dull.

By the time I graduated from high school, the account had grown. In college, when I worked in the summertime, I always paid myself first. I added small amounts to my account with every job. I could see that over those years my money was earning more and more in interest and that the interest was helping to earn even more. By the time I got married at twenty-three, I had saved enough to pay off all my husband's student loans. Otherwise, we might have started married life heavily in debt. By the time I left college, I was certain that consistent savings was important.

As a young married woman, I found saving much more difficult. We needed, or so we thought, so many things and our saving went out the window. The pay yourself first rule seemed to slip further and further away. I missed the sense of progress and security that a financial cushion gave me. As soon as I could, I started saving for my children so that they would understand the same lesson that I had learned: "I'd rather collect interest than pay it."

ASSETS VERSUS DEBT: "Compound interest is the eighth wonder of the free world, and you can't get any of it without some savings." Sam Potter

Note: I wonder if schools still offer passbook savings for kids. I know that it was not available for my children at the schools they attended. Maybe we should bring it back. Our schools have not served us well in educating us about financial matters. Financial ignorance creates painful stress in marriages and a painful adulthood. Ignorance of money and how it works is the curse we place on our children. Without financial education, we as adults must learn to survive in a financially driven world without the benefit of basic tools. Because our schools do not teach the "Economic Game of Life" as a central part of the curriculum, we condemn our children to learn about money in the school of hard knocks.

The figures for personal bankruptcy in our current economy are frightening proof that we have educated our society poorly. The lack of retirement funding is a savings and investment problem. It is a time bomb waiting to happen. The longer we delay the process of becoming a proficient investor, the more skilled an investor we must become in order to make up for the loss of time.

When we marry or leave home to go out on our own, we launch a huge future need for cash. We need to acquire the "stuff" to set up a homestead. Add to that basic need a societal unwillingness to accept personal responsibility, and you have a formula for anger and envy. This anger can be directed toward the system, the government, or anyone financially better off. In many ways the anger is justified because our education system does not teach children the rules of the economic game of life early enough for them to truly learn how to play. Their parents are supposed to do that. What happens to the children of the children who were never taught? The longer you wait to play by the financial rules of life, the harder it is to win. See Appendixes C and D.

It's so difficult to save money
when your neighbors keep buying things
you can't afford!

–E. C. McKenzie

A Day Late and a Dollar Short

Financial Readiness

I stormed into the house and slammed the front door. As it smacked closed, I saw the chandelier shake. I knew I was in trouble. I didn't realize I was still so mad. Taking out your temper on others or on the property of others wasn't allowed in the Potter household, and I had just done that. If Mom or Dad heard that slam, I was going to get a lecture on conduct.

I was just coming to grips with my actions when I heard Dad heading toward me from the back of the house.

"What in blazes is going on? Suzanne Potter, are you going to tear the house down?" he asked.

Sheepishly, I muttered something like, "I'm sorry, Daddy. I didn't realize how mad I was at myself."

"Why in the world are you mad at yourself, little girl? Take it easy on yourself; the house will be grateful."

"It's not funny, Dad. I saw this wonderful dress downtown today. It was on sale for fifty percent off, just for the day. It would be perfect for Easter, and I even have shoes to match and everything."

"Well, why didn't you get it or put it on hold?"

"They wouldn't let me put it on hold, and it was a one-day sale anyway. What makes me really mad was that June and I had eaten lunch right before I found it. June said she would loan me all the money she had on her, but by the time we counted out all our money we were still more than a dollar short. It made me madder than ever to be so close and lose out for a lousy dollar!"

Dad started to laugh. "So you're telling me that you were 'a day late and a dollar short.'"

"It's not funny, Daddy! It was a great buy. Now that I know I could have bought the dress for 50 percent off, I could never be happy with it if I had to pay full price."

Dad stopped laughing and scrunched his brow. "Well, it's best if you can just try to put it behind you as an opportunity lost. There will be other opportunities, and this won't be the last one you'll miss in life. It's far easier than you think to spot a great opportunity and see it too late to take advantage of it, or to not have enough money saved to do it. Don't worry about this one. Just keep your eyes peeled for the next opportunity. It will show up. Nobody enjoys being 'a day late and a dollar short.'"

I headed upstairs to my bedroom to mourn my loss alone. It was a beautiful dress. He didn't understand. How could he?

But, I didn't want to understand him either.

FINANCIAL READINESS: An opportunity can pass you by if you are too late in recognizing it. You can also miss out on an opportunity because you don't have the financial ability to take advantage of what you see.

God gives every bird his worm,
but he does not throw it into the nest.

–P. D. James

The Early Bird Catches the Worm

Maximizing Return

*I*t was a Sunday summer night, and it was getting late. As usual, I did not want Dad to leave in the morning. I wanted him to stay home with me and play. I wanted Dad to be on summer vacation, too. I begged him not to go to work the next morning.

As I talked, I could tell that I was not going to convince Dad to stay home and play with me. It was his job to provide for Sammy Junior, Mom, and me. Dad was going to have to go to work whether I wanted him to or not.

Not to be dissuaded, I tried a new strategy. Maybe Dad could leave late and have breakfast with Sammy Junior and me before he left? It was about then that I got my first exposure to the Ben Franklin and Sam Potter wisdom of "the early bird catches the worm."

Daddy said that he had to get up at 3:00 A.M. in the morning so that he could be in Waco by 5:30 A.M. to start making calls on the cobblers. Most of his buyers were little mom-and-pop-owned shoe repair shops. Dad's customers had to work long, hard hours to earn a living.

Dad said the best time to talk to them about buying the supplies they needed was *before* they opened the shop for business.

Dad understood and liked his customers. In his view, the way to generate an order was to be at the customer's store before opening, early in the morning. He did not want to interfere with his customers' livelihood and take their valuable income-generating time.

Dad put his customers' needs above his own. His commitment to his customers is probably why Dad was Potts-Knaur's top-producing salesman. Although I was very young, I learned to appreciate the work ethic of my father. I never consciously recognized that my young brain was developing a picture of success. Dad was a role model of commitment and diligence long before I knew what those words meant. He was teaching me that financial rewards are out there in our society, but it is not a "free lunch" world. Those who want financial rewards have to get up and get moving. I was beginning to understand that "the early bird catches the worm" meant timely action gets results, but at a deeper level, I received the clear implication that the late bird might get nothing at all.

After I started my own family and began to worry about retirement, I learned how to use a financial calculator. I was astonished with what I learned about the advantages of early savings. Without a financial calculator, the numbers didn't possess the same reality. As I played with my HP-12C calculator and projected annual savings compounding at different rates of returns over a variable time frame, I convinced myself that no great rate of return could compare to the benefits of lifelong investing and compounding. Investing early and often was the easiest and most certain way to fund later life retirement. Starting delays of only a few years made success less reliable. Dad was right again about the benefits of being an early bird. It is true on the job, and it is true in building financial freedom.

MAXIMIZING RETURN: The early bird proverb is true in building a retirement fund, in growing a business, and in advancing a career. See Appendixes C and D.

Money Won't Come to You; You Have To Go to It

Entitlement

*I*t was a very hot summer day, and Sammy Junior and I were on our way to Waco for our summer visit. Dad was taking us to spend a week with Ginny Ma, Mother's mother, and Tino, our step-grandfather. Sammy Junior and I loved to visit Ginny Ma and Tino. It would be a week of having the big red rooster crow and wake us up at sunup. We would chase fireflies at night and catch them and put them in a jar. In the evening, we would make ice cream out on the back stoop and watch Ginny Ma brush and groom Lady, a beautiful collie dog.

Since Dad was a traveling salesman, Sammy Junior and I were going to make business calls with him until we got to Ginny Ma's. We had stopped in West, a small German town about halfway between Dallas and Waco. It was 1948 or '49, and air-conditioning was not in the home or in any of the cars. We got up at 4 A.M. to dress and leave Dallas. We got to West very early, and Dad told Sammy Junior and me to wait in the car parked in the shade. In today's violent society, it would be unthinkable to leave children in an open car, but it was the norm in the '40s and '50s. It also was no more uncomfortable sitting in an open car than it was going into the unair-conditioned cobbler shops. Most of the time we were cooler than the adult workers shut inside the buildings.

Sammy Junior and I were to color in our coloring books until Dad finished his work. By the time Dad came out, it was close to ten or eleven, and all I remember is that it was hot. A Texas summer without a breeze is really something. Before air-conditioning came along, there was no relief until fall.

Dad came and got us. He took us down to the drug store at the corner for an ice cream soda. We were grumpy and cross from waiting so long in the hot car. Everywhere you looked, the heat seemed to rise off the sidewalks and streets in waves.

I remember asking Daddy, "Why can't we just go straight to Ginny Ma's?"

Dad said, "I've got to make my sales calls on the way down to Waco. There are only a few more to go until we get to Waco."

The thought of being bored once again as we waited for Dad gave rise to another round of complaints. About then, Dad explained with his characteristic brevity: "Money won't come to you, kids; you have to go to it."

"I don't understand, Daddy. What do you mean?" I asked a bit confused.

"Well, kids, when people are trying to earn money for their families, they have to figure out what it is that they can do that someone will be willing to pay for. Some types of work will pay more money than other types of work. For me, sales made the most sense because that way I could increase my income if I did an extra good job. When you are trying to earn a living, you have to go and do what the customer needs. If the customer doesn't get his needs met, then he won't give you and your company any money. No sale, no exchange of money. That is universal. Without somebody selling the product, money doesn't change hands. Just like I have to go out and find the customers so that the company and I make money, Mr. Potts has to show up every business day to make sure that the orders I create get filled. Companies are just a bunch of people on the same team; each person has a job to do to make it all fit together. That way everyone gets paid. Making money takes effort; it won't just drop in your lap." Dad smiled and looked us in the eyes to make sure we followed what he had said.

"Does that mean when I get grown I'll have to go out and work, too?" I asked because I knew Mom did not work. She stayed home with us.

"Well, for Sammy Junior the answer is definitely yes because he is going to have to earn enough to take care of himself at the very minimum. For you Suzie, the answer is not as clear. Whether you have to work full-time will depend on whether you are single or married and also what your family needs most—you at home or you working for a paycheck. That unknown need for you, little girl, means that you need to be fully prepared to take care of yourself no matter what happens. Money won't come to you, any more than it will come to your brother. You both are going to have to learn how to go and get it for yourselves and your families."

ENTITLEMENT: To make a lot of money you must put forth the energy to make it happen.

Jack-of-All-Trades, Master of None

Focus

$\mathcal{E}$arl Dee stood in the doorway, clothed in a white undershirt beneath black-and-white-striped baggy overalls. His curly black hair needed combing, and his hands, face, and clothes were smeared with some kind of smelly motor oil. I had only seen Earl Dee once before, and he had that same pungent oily smell then, too.

Earl Dee was Dad's brother, but he was a stranger to Sammy Junior and me. Earl Dee wasn't at all like Dad. Earl Dee was a handyman, and Dad was as unhandy as you can get. Earl Dee was quiet and somewhat shy. Dad was outgoing and funny. It was confusing to me, because they did not seem like brothers.

Earl Dee didn't say much; he just went about the job of building a sandbox and a big swing set for Sammy Junior and me to play on. Dad never spoke about his family. For Earl Dee to show up out of nowhere was bewildering.

It was an awesome swing set, one of the biggest ones I had ever seen outside a school playground. Big blocks of concrete anchored it, so three children could swing to the highest trees and never risk a tilt. Earl Dee was indeed a handy man!

I remember asking Mom if Earl Dee was a salesman like Dad. She said no, that Earl Dee did odd jobs for a living. She said he needed work, so Dad offered to pay him to build us a swing set. Mom said that Earl Dee had never married, and he was sort of a jack-of-all-trades.

Isn't it funny the things you remember and later link together as you grow up? I knew Earl Dee as a jack-of-all-trades. It wasn't until later that I heard the rest of the popular phrase: "jack-of-all-trades, master of none."

The subtle impact of that thought played in my subconscious. Later, it became a special stimulus to me. When I knew I needed to focus and master something, I remembered the musty smell of motor oil and greasy clothes was somehow linked to choices that Earl Dee had made. Dad and Earl Dee seemed so different in almost every way. If it weren't for the Potter features that they both had, I would never have believed them kin. I knew that Earl Dee was barely getting by in life, and that Dad was helping him out. Here were two brothers whose life choices had taken them on very different paths. The only conclusion I could derive was not to become a jack-of-all-trades and master of none.

I would follow my dad's path.

Focus: Different choices create different lifestyles. We all choose. The only difference is that some people focus on the result of the choice; others focus on the choice itself. We must focus on both. To achieve contentment with your chosen field of work, you must weigh the pluses and minuses of the work, along with the pluses and minuses of the pay.

There was a time when a fool
and his money were soon parted.
Now it happens to everybody.

—E. C. McKenzie

A Fool and His Money Are Soon Parted

Financial Responsibility

I was in junior high, and my English assignment was to write a paper about my dad. The teacher, in an effort to stimulate thought, had given us some ideas on questions that we might want to ask our fathers for our reports.

When Dad came home Friday night for the weekend, I asked him what kind of business he was in. Dad loved to cut up and tease, so it didn't surprise me when he said, "I'm in the money business." I remember groaning, "Daddy, I'm serious." Immediately, with a big grin on his face, he said, "Well, so am I, Sissy."

"You sell leather goods, don't you? So that is your business, isn't it?" I said, struggling to get back on track.

Then Dad gave me the real answer. "No, Suzie, selling is how I get our money. But I'm in the money business."

I was confused and irritated. I didn't want to write this paper anyway, and here Dad was making it harder than it had to be.

"My job is to earn enough money so that we can have food to

eat, a roof over our heads, clean clothes to wear, and a safe place to sleep at night. My job isn't just to earn the money, but it is also to earn and save enough money so that you and Sammy Junior can go to college, something I never got to do. No, Sissy, my business is making the money and managing the money. In this day and age, making money isn't enough. You've got to learn how to keep and grow your money.

"Money is an important thing to have when times are tough. It is harder to hang onto money than it is to make money, and that in itself can be plenty of hard work. There are people waiting to take away your hard-earned money, and it is easy to get taken in. When you're in the money business, it pays to learn all you can, because a fool and his money are soon parted."

FINANCIAL RESPONSIBILITY: Financial responsibility is not about the job or the size of the paycheck. Financial responsibility is about being in the business of building assets to provide for your family needs, current and future. Managing your money to make the most of it is one of the most important skills you can learn.

There's No Such Thing as a Free Lunch

Self-Reliance

*M*om, Dad, Sammy Junior, and I pulled off the road in Waco, Texas. At last we were going to the Chicken Shack. Every summer as we returned from our annual vacation to Port Aransas, we begged Dad to time our drive home so that we could eat at the Chicken Shack. Nobody in the state served up better fried chicken, mashed potatoes, cream gravy, and steaming hot yeast rolls ready for a big dose of honey than the Chicken Shack. Even the fried gizzards were to die for. In fact, the gizzards were my absolute favorite.

Stuffed to the gills with a meal that lived up to our memories, we headed back to the car in the hot Texas sun. As Sammy Junior and I hopped in the backseat, Mom said, "Aren't you kids going to thank your dad for a great meal? Where are your manners?"

"Thank you, Daddy," we chimed.

"You're welcome, kids," he grinned. "Your mom wants you to remember to mind your manners. But I want you to remember: there is no free lunch!"

"What are you talking about, Dad?" I asked.

"Whenever you get anything in life, someone had to produce it. Even if it's free, wild blackberries like we picked on the side of the road yesterday, we still had to do the work of picking them. We all traded our vacation time for blackberries. We could have been at the beach instead.

"Kids, nobody gets off scot-free in this life. We all are trading time or money for what we want. Today, I paid the bill for you because I love you. But you mark my words, there will be a day when nobody but you will be there to pay the bill. It's just part of being a grown-up."

Dad turned on the car engine, and, as we drove off, I wondered what I would need to learn so one day my time would be worth something.

SELF-RELIANCE: How do you prepare yourself to pay the bills for the time when no one else is willing to pay them for you? Learn to appreciate the value of your money and your time. Make the most of both.

A lazy person, whatever the talents
with which he set out,
will have condemned himself to second-hand
thoughts and second-hand friends.

–Cyril Connolly

Don't Be a Deadbeat

Self-Indulgence

"**S**uzanne Potter, get up off that sofa. Turn off the TV and go clean up the bathroom like your mother told you to. Quit trying to mooch off your mother. You think if you sit still long enough, then she'll do your work for you."

Surprised and confused, I said, "What do you mean by mooch, Daddy?"

He answered, "A mooch is someone who is not willing to pull their own weight. They would rather let other people do all of their work for them. We've got too many moochers nowadays. Moochers are deadbeats, too lazy to work. They are either too lazy to get up off their behinds and do physical labor, or they are too lazy to spend the hard time at learning in order to earn a living doing mental labor. There is no excuse for a moocher.

"Don't misunderstand, Suzie. Anyone can get down on their luck now and then. That's okay, and we should all try to help them out. But they've got to do their part. Moochers and deadbeats won't even try to do what they can. They just think they are too good and that the world owes them a living. Pure laziness! Just the way you are acting about that bathroom. So get up and get after it, and quit mooching off your mom!"

I was sixteen and I was mooching.

SELF-INDULGENCE: We all must learn that life is not a free ride. We must shoulder our share of the physical labor at home, as well as take on our share of the financial load as we mature.

Time Is Money

Time Is the Value

*W*e all want a quality lifestyle. How we define that quality of life varies from person to person. Most of us grow weary when life is just about surviving from day to day. We long for more. One of the reasons so many of us feel that we are part of the "rat race" is that we don't seem to get ahead financially. We have been taught to raise the bar on the level of survival just about the time we begin to advance financially. We are too busy buying status instead of peace of mind.

In order to manage our lives and achieve all of the things we want in life, we must get clear on how economic value is created. Time is the currency of life, not money. The availability of our time is a diminishing personal resource. When we are born, we have 100% of our lifetime ahead of us. With every passing day, our remaining time decreases. At birth our ability to trade our supply of time for money is theoretically zero, because as an infant we don't possess any marketable skills. As each of us moves forward through time, our actions, lack of action, and luck determine how much money someone else will pay to have ownership of that which is ours, our time.

When we look for a job, we are selling a piece of our life to the highest bidder. What is an hour of your time worth? We can do nothing to increase the market value of one hour of our life, or we can do a great deal to enhance its perceived value to others. The choice begins at birth and ends at death.

Time is the commodity we barter for survival. Money is just the currency of the trade. Money merely provides liquidity. The skills we develop, the economic need for those skills, and how well we sell the value of those skills determines how much currency we are given for the use of our personal skill set.

We can sell our time, or we can utilize it ourselves. When we utilize it ourselves, we either spend it, or we invest it. We can spend our time sitting, daydreaming, reading, playing, or visiting. We can invest our time in study, learning, or helping others. The use of our time can only be defined as a profitable investment if the end result of that study, learning, and giving elevates the resale value of our time. If we study and learn and never create added economic value to our time, then we should conclude that we have "spent" the time not "invested" the time.

I did not understand all these principles as a young woman, but my dad made certain that I understood the underlying simple concepts at an early age. He began when I was very young by just making the phrase "time is money" a part of his dialogue. I remember packing for a vacation and to speed our packing, Dad came into the bedroom and said, "Time is a wasting, kids, and time is money. We need to get on the road." As a child, I did not recognize that Dad was inserting fundamental financial concepts subtly into our young minds. To this day, I am not sure if it was conscious teaching on Dad's part or not.

Perhaps these lessons were so much of his own philosophy that it just naturally flowed into his daily speech. As we grew, Dad was inclined to add to this basic premise. The summer before I left for college, Dad expanded this teaching.

It was summertime and Mom had the big ice cream freezer out to make ice cream. We were all anxious to hear the motor on the ice cream freezer grind to a halt. Mom's delicious homemade vanilla was on the other side of the noise.

As we all sat down to eat, I asked, "Daddy, what should I take at college? I don't know what I want to do or what I want to be when I get out of school."

"Well, Suzie, I hope you'll get yourself a degree in business. The main reason I wanted you to go to college is to increase the value of your work skills and your understanding of business. Unless you want to be a doctor or an engineer, I think you ought to get a business degree, and I hope you take accounting because it is important to every business. Accounting is the language of business. Someday, you may even want to have your own business. The higher the level of skills you develop the more you will get paid for your time. The more valuable your time, the fewer hours you will have to work to cover your basic needs. Skills give you options that let you earn more or work less, whichever you choose. If you don't acquire skills with economic value, then you have little choice but to work all the time just to survive."

As Dad finished, I said, "I guess I understand. I might as well major in business as anything else." I pretended to understand what Dad was trying to tell me, but truthfully, I only got the general point. Dad didn't care; all he wanted was for us to accept the broad concepts and life would teach us the rest.

We either sell our time for money, we spend, or we give it to others—it is our choice. There is no intent on my part to declare a choice right or wrong. The point is to act with wisdom and clarity because time is not free. Time has a cost. Time costs you if your time spent in some manner could be exchanged for money. It may be well worth the price. Just recognize that there is a cost.

The financial game of life begins with the knowledge that time is the fundamental commodity we exchange for money. Good use of time can put money in your pocket. Leverage your time spent so that you win financially. Bad use of time can take money out of your pocket for the remainder of your life.

TIME IS THE VALUE: An hour of unskilled labor has little economic value in the workplace, since any warm body can be substituted. The worker who chooses not to acquire skills does so at his own loss.

A Full Day's Work for a Full Day's Pay

Money Follows Value

"*I*t was my first real summer job. As I was getting
ready to leave the house with Mom to report for my first day on the
job, Dad walked to the front of the house and yelled out,
"Remember, Suzie, always give your boss 'A full day's work for a full
day's pay'; don't be doing any goofing off on company time."

I called back, "I won't forget, Daddy; bye, I'll see you later."

It wasn't as if I had just heard this for the first time. Dad's
hard work ethic was part of my socialization as a child. He was a big
advocate for going the extra mile. Dad was not his own boss but a
commissioned employee when he instructed my brother and me to
"always deliver more value to any job than you take." His guidance
came long before I was old enough to know what a job was, much
less what a day's pay meant. Dad was instructing my brother and me
on work ethic as far back as I could remember. We were taught that
when we got a job, we should come early and stay late. Dad under-

stood that to advance, you had to give added value first. Compensation follows value; it does not precede it.

Giving precedes receiving. Dad understood this universal truth. I wonder how many young people are stuck without a hope of job advancement because they are only willing to deliver exactly what they are paid to do and nothing more.

Giving, as a concept, is missed in other areas of business as well, especially in commission sales. Sales and marketing people attend networking events to promote sales. They go looking for a lead. Most traditional networking events prove unproductive because few attendees truly understand the principle of giving as a requisite for receiving. Sales professionals would do well to look deeper into a concept that the network marketing industry has understood for decades. Give leads and you will get them. The greatest reward in any area of life is in giving more that you get.

It is fascinating that Dad understood these very contemporary concepts. Dad's wisdom didn't come out of a self-help book or seminar. Bookstores were nowhere to be found, and self-help books were as obscure as a diamond mine. The universal principle, to first give to receive, is scriptural and as old as time. Yet, this universal truth is often misunderstood even by the well educated.

From the time I was a very little girl, Dad was telling me that America was a great country and that anyone could become anything they wanted to become. Daddy's formula for success was to work hard, create a strategy, and put your mind and effort into your dreams.

Money Follows Value: The way to make more money is to create more value. Money follows value, not the other way around.

Make your money first— then think about
spending it is the best of all possible credos,
for the man who wishes to succeed.
A sense of thrift is essential for success . . .

–J. Paul Getty

Pay Yourself First
Discipline of Accumulation

"Show me your check, little girl," Dad said as he finished dinner. I pushed my plate aside and ran up to my room and grabbed the envelope with my first paycheck. One of Mom's friends helped me get a summer job downtown at the Tower Theater. The movie Gigi was going to run all summer. Tickets were sold by reservation, and the seats were assigned, much like the musical productions of today.

I was between my junior and senior year in high school, and I was hired as an usher for the summer. It was a fun job, so I was thrilled. I had worked two weeks, and today was my first payday. I don't remember how much the check was for, but I remember that I was excited about getting paid.

"Here it is," I said, as I shoved it proudly in front of Dad.

Dad spent a minute or two looking at it and smiled. "It looks like you done good, little girl. What are you going to pay yourself?"

I was embarrassed because I knew he was talking about putting some money in my savings account. Saving my big, first check was not what I had been thinking about. I thought about all the fun my friends and I could have shopping the downtown sales for clothes. I knew how much Dad loved me, and I never wanted to disappoint him, so I looked him straight in the eye and said, " I haven't thought about it yet, Daddy. What do you think I should do with it?"

"Well, Sissy, how much you save is your decision. It is, after all, your money, and what you do with it is your business. But I've learned that the only way to get an edge on life is to pay yourself first. The more money you feel comfortable setting aside, the sooner your life will get comfortable financially. Compound interest is the eighth wonder of the free world, and you can't get any of it without some savings."

Dad never dictated how much I should save. He saw decision making as a part of growing up. He knew he had to let me feel my own way. He gave direction, but it was up to me to use or not use his advice. I had a small savings, but this was the first time I had "big" money. That day I made my decision to add part of my paycheck to my savings account every payday. Dad never double-checked to see what I was doing. I was on my own, only accountable to me.

Most of us know we must start a disciplined savings plan, but we procrastinate and fail to start. Unfortunately, there are many adults who were not taught as children to plan for their future. Most Americans live with a short-term plan. "Pay yourself first" was the first thing my dad taught me about a long-term financial strategy. Most Americans never take the first step, and then they wonder why they cannot get ahead financially.

Dad said, "You can't tell how much money a man has in his bankbook by the shoes he wears, the car he drives, or the house he lives in. A lot of millionaires don't care what the Joneses think, own, or do. They just keep on working to keep the wolf away from the door." He told me, "If you were to go downtown at lunch break, H. L. Hunt could walk right past you and you'd never know it. He'd be walking alone, not riding, carrying his lunch in a brown paper bag, and probably wearing a rumpled suit. Real wealth usually isn't about show. There are some exceptions, but most of the time people are too busy trying to work and do the best they can to worry about what someone else is thinking."

If you want to find out how to get away from staying broke and move into a more comfortable lifestyle, learn from those who have done it. Dad would be the first to tell you it is hard work and the lazy don't get there, but it is definitely doable with discipline. Dad would tell you if he were still alive, "Stop listening to your broke friends. They know how to be broke. Some of them are experts at it. Just ask them."

Since most broke people do not know anyone wealthy, how can they learn? Get some books about the wealthy and study them. Read *The Millionaire Next Door* by Stanley and Danko. Read and reread all of Robert Kiyosaki's books: *Rich Dad Poor Dad, Cashflow Quadrant, Rich Dad Poor Dad's Guide to Investing,* and *Smart Kid Rich Kid.*

Accumulated capital gives you financial options. "Pay yourself first" is one of those things my dad preached. Saying this was not enough; Dad had to start me on the course with my first paycheck. This lesson was the most economically valuable lesson my father ever taught me. Saving is very difficult without this strategy.

Did I learn it well? No. Did I do it early and always? Early, yes. Always, no.

My execution has been sloppy over the years. But in the last fifteen years, I have done a better job. Dad said that mastering the art of saving and investing was the secret to a comfortable lifestyle. He proved the model, and I never question a cook with a recipe that works.

Discipline of Accumulation: If you don't pay yourself first, nobody else will. The future arrives before you know it, and the time to start planning is now. See Appendixes B, C and D.

God made man.
Then He stepped back, looked,
and said, "I can do better than that."

–Erma Bombeck

Girl Talk

Women and Money

*W*hen I was growing up, I frequently had a group of girlfriends over to play or to visit. If Dad accidentally entered the den or living room when we were there, he would always say, "Didn't mean to interrupt your girl talk."

We "played" until we were thirteen. After that, we graduated to the status of teenager. Girlfriends no longer came over to "play." They came over to "visit." It never occurred to me back then that girl talk was distinctly different from boy talk. Or even more relevant than that, girl talk was distinctly different from talking man-to-man. Dad's distinction let me know that female conversation was in fact different.

Have you ever noticed that when a group of men get together for lunch, they talk about sports, women, or money? When women get together, they talk about food, family, entertainment, men, clothes, or decorating—rarely money.

Why is it that women earn less than men? Seventy-five cents

on the dollar, yet, over their longer life expectancy, women will need more money than the average man. In spite of these well-known facts, we do not want to "worry our pretty little heads" about money. If you are female, and forty or older, you have been told this or at least heard it said frequently. Do the words "pretty little head" subtly imply our lack of comparable ability? Don't misunderstand—as a young, adult female, I was never a bra-burning feminist. I have, however, observed the absence of female role models in the areas of wealth creation, management, and business.

If there is "a good old girl's society," it certainly has been off the radar until very recently. Women historically have not shown an interest in helping a "sister" in the area of business. We help each other in other ways, but when it comes to money and business it is as though we do not understand. This attitude seems to be changing. Until we as women adopt the belief that we do have to worry our "pretty little heads" about our financial future, we will continue to experience mediocre financial lives. Worry today or you will surely have pain tomorrow. That is a promise.

Little heads produce little results, whether they are pretty or not. Little heads will maintain little pocketbooks. Until we learn to talk straight, "woman-to-woman" about our financial situations and create solutions and a support network, we will never develop the synergies for wealth that have been created by the "good old boy's network."

Men build financial fraternities, where they develop trusted relationships, and the price of admission is contribution. The best financial fraternities are those with the most money and the brightest minds. It is an ever-changing spiral of who you know and what can you do.

As "good old girls," we must make up for lost time. We need to openly share investment ideas and advice. We need to refer one another to like-minded individuals the way the men have done for decades. After all, there are more "old girls" than "old boys." Now is the time to redefine ourselves for our financial future and our children's future.

WOMEN AND MONEY: "Girl talk" needs to become more informational, more instructional, more supportive, more mentoring, and more focused on areas of financial opportunity. Create a network of female financial helpmates today.

Timing Is Everything
Timing

*I*t was July 20, 1969, and we had bought a new color TV. It was our first step up from the traditional black-and-white model. The purchase was specifically to see the live broadcast of the NASA Apollo flight and the first walk on the moon. If we were going to put a man on the moon and simulcast the event, then it was worth moving up our spending budget to witness in full color Neil Armstrong's historic moonwalk.

Time has dimmed the details, but the excitement, anxiety, and disbelief that swirled through my brain is still vivid. Only a few years earlier, President Kennedy had set a national goal to beat the Russians to land a man on the moon. Few had dared to set such an ambitious goal. Everyone knew that the Russians had made much more progress in space exploration than we had, but once the President had set that goal, our energy and belief were directed toward making the dream a reality.

It was amazing to me how much had transpired in the few

years between JFK having set the goal and that momentous day. We installed the TV. We prepared to watch and wait. We had no idea what to expect, but before we knew it, there was Armstrong stepping out on the surface of the moon. Amazing.

It changed everything. One well-timed event changed attitudes throughout our country overnight. Fears that we had fallen behind the Russians in technology were set aside. Fears that the Americans had lost their will to achieve were dispelled. Concerns that we could win the long struggle against Communism were eased. Our belief in ourselves and pride in our nation were reignited at a single moment in time.

Yes, there are definitely moments when the timing of achievement is critical. I saw it as a young mother in the moon landing, and I see it in my own life, and in the lives of others. Dad emphasized how important timing is in the results that play out in our lives.

When I was little, Dad would frequently point to a decision he made on December 6, 1941, to validate "timing is everything." Dad told me that late in 1941 he was a young salesman with Potts-Knaur Leather Company, and he felt that the war in Europe with Hitler was escalating to dangerous levels. He knew that the war could easily spread and pull the United States into the battle. He reasoned that if that occurred, American goods would be diverted to the war effort and one of the things that might be in short supply was tires.

Since Dad made his living driving across Texas and Oklahoma, he could see that a scarcity of tires might impede his ability to feed his family. So on Saturday, December 6, 1941, he invested in an extra set of brand-new tires for his car and stored them under the bed. The next morning, the United States was at war. As it turned out, he worked throughout the war here at home. Amazed at his fortunate timing, he never forgot that decision.

"Timing is everything. Don't neglect its importance, Sissy."

For today's teenagers, timing is more critical than it has ever been. Holding off childbearing until after completing an education is one of the most important timing issues for teens; yet, our society continues to send mixed messages.

We project sexual encounters as the acceptable norm in sit-coms and movies. We allow the media to brainwash our young men and women. They are made to believe that if they are not sexually active, then they are in the minority and old-fashioned and out-of-date. It is difficult to imagine a more dangerous message than one that advocates promiscuity. Promiscuity increases AIDS among our teens, and it increases the risk that our young girls will become mothers before they have had the opportunity to equip themselves with the educational skills they need for financial survival.

What are we adults doing to protect our families from society's destructive values? Our only hope is to teach our own children that timing is, in fact, critical. Lack of preparation for retirement by our aging population is equally dangerous. Negative saving rates in our country document the adult indifference toward monthly savings. In saving, where compounding can be so empowering, early commitment is fundamental to a successful accumulation strategy.

The importance of timing in business is well recognized. There is a time when a new business idea appears too soon; too far ahead of its time. When that happens, it is extremely difficult to develop a market. There is also a time when a business idea is too late to market. Either someone else has filled your niche, or the window of opportunity has come and gone.

Survival depends on how and when corporations respond to the unexpected. When a business produces a bad product or creates a public danger, decisions must be swift. If the response is prompt, even if it incurs loss, the consumer will respond positively. Delay protecting the customer, and the business continues at its own peril.

The quick recalls of the cyanide tampering of Tylenol and the defective Intel Pentium chips were appropriately timed business responses. Ford and Firestone delayed recalling defective tires in 2000. Insensitive to their markets, they are paying a price for slow and improper judgment.

There are hundreds of books written on the significance that timing plays in the area of investing. As with so many things in life, the timing of our personal, business, and investing decisions impact everything else that follows.

TIMING: There are some events in life that later is too late and now is too soon. Get the timing right; it is crucial.

Time is more valuable than money.
You can get more money,
but you can't get more time.

–Jim Rohn

The Longer You Wait,
the More It's Going To Cost You

Price of Laziness

*I*t was a hot summer day, and Dad and Al Davis were playing cards and shooting the bull. As I entered the room, Dad laughed and hollered out, "The longer you wait, the more it is going to cost you." Al Davis really wasn't our uncle, but Dad had introduced Al to my daughters and told them to just call him "Uncle Al."

Al and his wife, Janie, owned a small lake house across the dirt road from Dad's. If Dad and Uncle Al were playing cards with one of my girls, the game of choice was Gin Rummy, Poker, High Low Jick Jack and the Game, or Go Fish. It didn't matter; soon after the game began, the fun started. Verbal jabs were part of it.

Indecision in life is the most costly lesson of all. Dad said it first, and I learned it much later. As I aged, life experiences began to pull together the proverbs of my childhood. Time completed the jigsaw puzzle and united all the pieces in a clearer vision.

"The longer you wait, the more it is going to cost you" is advice that applies to so many important decisions. One of the most important is the one to study hard and learn. If, in our youth, we fail to apply ourselves in serious study, it costs us ultimately in one way or another. The irony of this choice is that for most of us, studying is not fun. Learning can be hard work. It is easier to disengage our brain and allow a movie or TV to lead our mind away from work or thought.

As children we think we are getting away with something by avoiding all the hard work. The sad truth is, the longer you wait to educate yourself, the more it is going to cost you. I have observed the kids who avoid the hard work early on; they are the very ones that pay the biggest price. They may never equip themselves with the marketable tools they need to be highly paid for their work. We all must work or benefit from the work of someone else, if we expect to survive.

The quality of that survival is usually determined by how soon we start to equip ourselves with the knowledge the marketplace requires. That knowledge, if converted to skill, can create an income for you and your family. School is not the only teacher, but school is one of the best places to start acquiring skills. It is particularly sad to see so many young teens trying to skip out on education, as though it were a waste of time. Oddly enough, early learning is the best investment a young person can make. While I do not believe it is ever too late in life to start a new direction, I do believe that Dad was right in that "The longer you wait, the more it is going to cost you."

PRICE OF LAZINESS: Accept the wisdom that the cost of being lazy goes up over time. The sooner you begin educating yourself, the easier life becomes. Resist education and life becomes very difficult financially.

Avoiding danger is no safer in the long run
than outright exposure.
The fearful are caught as often as the bold.

–Helen Keller

Nothing Ventured, Nothing Gained

Risk and Reward

"**D**addy, can we talk?" I asked anxiously.

"Sure, Suzie, what do you want to talk about?" he asked.

"Well, several of my friends at school have been talking to me about maybe running for the student council. I'm not sure if I should or not," I said, simply stating my concern.

"Well, my first question is, is this something you would enjoy doing?"

"I think so. It is really an honor, and I think it would be fun," was my response.

"Then you have your answer. If you already knew that, then why did you ask me? Do you know?" Dad was opening up the real problem.

"Well, what if I don't get elected?" I was voicing my real concern.

"I guess that someone else will serve. I'm not trying to be cute; but I am trying to help you put your fear where it belongs. I would be willing to bet that you think there is shame in losing an election. And I will tell you there is honor in the trying, win or lose. There is shame in not going for what you want. If you don't run, you'll never know what you missed. Even in losing, the visibility may help you win some other office you would like to have later. My advice is run. Nothing ventured, nothing gained." Dad was firm.

I ran, I lost, and I did not die. I learned that losing wasn't as bad as I had made it. Dad's wisdom taught me to fight my irrational fears and to be willing to take personal risk for the things I really wanted in life.

More than twenty years later as a young mother recently relocated to Fort Wayne, Indiana, my middle daughter Suzy came home from junior high school with the same question for me.

"What's bothering you, Suzy?" I asked as my middle daughter pushed open the back door and entered the kitchen with a frown on her face.

"I don't know, Mom. I mean, I'm not sure what I want to do," she answered.

"Maybe, you should start over and tell me what you are talking about," I asked, clearly puzzled.

"Well, I've only been going to school for three weeks and Randy, one of the boys in my math class, has collected a petition with twenty-five names on it to put me on the ballot to run for student council. I didn't even know he was doing it. In order to run for the student council, the kids have to file a petition signed by twenty-five students. The petition acts as a nomination for balloting. Randy didn't tell me anything about it until he had all the required signatures. Randy showed it to me today and asked me if I would run. Mom, I was so surprised; I didn't know what to say. I told him I would let him know tomorrow, and now I don't know what to do." Suzy spoke so fast that I could barely follow her, but she seemed relieved to have the problem out in the open.

"Would you like to be on the student council if you didn't have to run to get there? Or would you find the responsibilities boring and a drag?" I asked, watching her closely as she responded.

"Well, yes, it would be fun and an honor to be a part of that group, but I am brand new in the school and new to Indiana and nobody knows me. So how could I possibly get elected?"

"Suzy, I only asked you if you would like the job, not whether or not winning was possible. We really need to think about these things separately, don't you agree? What we know so far is that 'yes' you would like it if you had the job; but you're not sure if you want to try to get what you want. Is that correct, so far?" I was trying to help Suzy think through her choices.

"I guess so. But what should I do, Mom?"

"Suzy, that really isn't something I should decide for you, but I will help you think about it. I tell you what; let's both sleep on this, and we will decide in the morning before you leave for school. Okay?" I asked.

"Okay, I guess," Suzy responded.

The next morning, I put coffee on to perk, and I was still unsure what I would say to Suzy. I was hoping that she had arrived at her own decision, independent of me. I went out to the mailbox and pulled out the morning paper. There on the front page was our answer.

Margaret Thatcher, called "The Iron Lady" by the press, was the British Prime Minister. Margaret Thatcher was secretly my heroine. She made me proud to be female. On the front page there was an article about Prime Minister Thatcher and her rise to power. Buried in the small print was the fact that Margaret Thatcher lost her first several runs for election. The message was clear. Where would Great Britain be if Margaret Thatcher had been afraid to lose?

When Suzy came down I had circled the article, and I told her to read it. Afterward she said, "I had already decided if Randy will be my campaign chairman, I'll give it a try."

I gave her a hug and said, "That sounds like a great idea. Just give it all you've got; don't do it half way."

Suzy won. She won more that an election. She won the courage to fail before a ballot was cast.

There is an allure to a safe, risk-free life because it removes fear and self-doubt from our minds, but the price for a life devoid of fear is high. Taking no risk is the highest risk of all.

Individuals seeking a risk-adverse life dominate our society. Avoiding risk is most heavily manifested in the transference of personal responsibility to others. If we take no personal responsibility for our decisions, then we run no risk of being wrong. Decision by consensus seems safe, free of criticism, and risk free. This type of nondecision allows our life to be controlled by others; there is no greater gamble than that.

How do we abandon our decision-making and what are the symptoms? Listen for phrases like, "Everybody does it," "Just go with the flow," or "Don't make waves." These phrases should notify us that we may be ceding our life to someone else's control—a life without thought, and devoid of self-determination.

God gave each of us our own brain to help us make our own decisions. How well we use our mind determines our life. It is the center of our personal creative force. Our ability to think is God's gift. Why are we so willing to assume the conclusions of others, rather than think of our own? If we willingly abdicate the use of our brains, then we are abandoning the person we could become. The choices others make for us will never reward us the way we could reward ourselves. Nothing creates a flatter life than one that blindly travels the paths others choose. Learn how to make your own decisions and take your own measured risks.

RISK AND REWARD: Rewards are rarely found in the safe decision. Rewards are found in assuming calculated risks, both personally and financially.

America Is the Land of Opportunity
Capitalism

*D*ad frequently professed his undying belief that America truly was a land full of opportunity. Dad said opportunity was accessible to anyone willing to work hard and develop the skills needed to take advantage of what was available. Five decades later, I was deeply involved in the wealth transformation of a man with drive and a dream.

My excitement was escalating as I tore the plastic cover from my *Forbes 400 Richest* issue dated October 14, 1996. I personally knew someone on the list, a certified billionaire, and I had helped him get there! I scanned the list quickly. I found the page and immediately turned to the picture and biography of Kenny Troutt, CEO of Excel Communications, Inc. There was Kenny, a child of the Illinois projects, transformed into an adult worth 1.4 billion dollars.

Forbes, in a later issue, would estimate that only 298 billionaires existed worldwide. One hundred forty-nine of those were American billionaires. Of those, many were self-made, first-generation wealth creators.

Opportunity is alive and attainable in America! A mixture of joy and pride filled my heart, as I sat down to study the list of American wealth creators. To create wealth you must use leverage. You can leverage your money through investments. You can leverage your time by building a business or growing an existing business. Building businesses created most of the wealth in America. To create wealth in business, you must create wealth for others in the form of jobs or returns on investment capital. The amount of wealth creation the very rich share and the way they contribute to a productive society varies. The truly rich do not get to the top alone. They develop a team of players. The team players share some of the wealth that is created through their commitment to the vision of the team leader. Many early loyal employees for Microsoft and Dell became multimillionaires. They chose to work for a wealth creator and assist in breathing life into the vision of their visionary leader.

All over America, independent representatives who had worked hard to make Excel one of the fastest growing companies in American history, were experiencing the same excitement that I was feeling. We experienced the proof of the "American Dream" firsthand.

Kenny had a vision for Excel. He saw a market opportunity, and he seized it. To bring that opportunity to life, he had to share the concept, build a working team, and deliver a benefit to the customer. By executing on all fronts, Troutt created services for the masses and an open opportunity to be on his team. As services were delivered and team players were compensated, his wealth evolved.

Kenny Troutt became a billionaire, and many others who helped build his early vision became millionaires. According to *Forbes*, Troutt was a billionaire and hundreds of thousands of representatives knew that they had an important role in making that happen. It was instructive, as well as exciting. Multilevel marketing is an entrepreneurial training ground. It is a training school with money attached. The experience renewed my pride in our country. I was proud of my fellow entrepreneurs and proud of Kenny. As I watched Kenny's story unfold, I began to appreciate other great pioneering wealth creators, such as Amway's Richard DeVos and Jay Van Andel, also first generation, self-made billionaires. Mary Kay Ash, a multimillionaire, was a woman whose pioneering efforts made a spectacular contribution to women who wanted to work their own business.

Coming close to individuals who have created great wealth opens your eyes to the magnitude of our capitalistic society. My exposure to new thoughts and creativity gave me renewed courage to pursue the American dream. I had a new curiosity about the wealth creators in America, both traditional and nontraditional. It was possible to become wealthy in ways that I had never considered. I wanted to understand how it was done. My hunger to understand this phenomenon of massive wealth creation had been awakened.

As I sat down with the *Forbes 400 Richest,* I started to read the brief biographies of those listed. Dad had been right about opportunity in this country. I wanted to know how the other 399 in the list had created their fortunes. As I read, I knew that all the fearmongers proclaiming it was too late to get rich were wrong. Many of the very rich were in fact self-created in a period of only a few decades.

A shift occurred in my thinking. I had never *really* believed that I could achieve wealth. I believed I could be affluent but not wealthy. That day, Kenny Troutt and *Forbes* proved to me that my limited beliefs, limited drive, and limited skills were the problems. As Dad knew, there was no limit to opportunity in America. If I *wanted* unlimited opportunities, I would have to remove my personal limitations one at a time.

With the bar raised, I had to turn the question inward to search for what I really wanted and what was I willing to do to achieve it.

CAPITALISM: We all accept on some level that America is a country full of opportunities, but very few of us understand that the financial limitations in our life are frequently self-imposed. Biographic evidence of phenomenal success is prolific. Many financial success stories started from a point of limited education and limited financial resources, but they never involved limited determination.

Luck to me is something else—hard work—
and realizing what is opportunity
and what isn't.

–Lucille Ball

I'd Rather Be Lucky than Smart

Opportunity

*D*ad peppered his language with philosophical meaning. His words were light. His message was profound. As a child, I could not distinguish between those expressions that were just fun for the moment and those that were fundamentally instructive. Dad deposited both playful and profound thoughts into my brain. Over time, their mysteries dissolved, and the profound words became instructive.

"I'd rather be lucky than smart" was a phrase that I frequently heard as a child; its meaning eluded me for most of my life. Since I knew I could do nothing about luck, I spent most of my life working on the things I could do something about. I worked on the knowledge part of that equation. Year after year, I slowly worked on improving my knowledge and financial understanding only to finally realize that what Dad meant by luck was not a pure random type of luck. So, for most of my life, I failed to explore and take advantage of the luck that my father said he would rather have.

My entrepreneurial father was talking about business opportunity. He was talking about the impact of timing on any economic opportunity. He was referring to being at the right place, at the right time, and with the ability and willingness to seize the moment and profit from it.

Daddy's, "I'd rather be lucky than smart," in my early adulthood didn't seem to help me. I misunderstood what he was saying; but once I realized he was talking about opportunity, I knew I could learn to look for that. Being lucky and locating a great opportunity is, by itself, not enough. You have to become smart enough to evaluate your luck and know what actions need to be taken.

Achievers work their entire adult lives in areas where they can get smarter and more skilled. Luck, however, is something rarely considered. To find good opportunities, we have to groom our thinking to look toward the future. Most of us apply ourselves to known endeavors, but opportunity generally sits out in front of a new field or in an economic shift. Seeing opportunity is not like learning facts. It is visualizing the future course of events and attempting to forecast or influence how they will play out. In other words, we must look ahead and place ourselves in front of a timely opportunity or trend.

Implicit in seizing opportunity is the need for *courage* to follow your convictions and the *ability* to place a large bet on that conviction. These can be high-risk areas that present a great deal of discomfort to the average person. To be in front of an opportunity is not for the faint of heart. It frequently means that few see what you see, and that can cause a great deal of personal anxiety when you seem to be a consensus of one. The problem with opportunity is that when the consensus recognizes it, it is usually too late.

I found that I also had an overly simplified view of pure luck. Winning the lottery is luck, but what are the odds of winning? The odds are horrible, but they don't matter if you don't buy a ticket. Without the action of buying the ticket, even "pure luck" cannot work. Luck requires that we take some appropriate action. It was my early mistake to believe that luck was a passive occurrence. The real difference between luck and opportunity is the odds. In luck we have no influence on the outcome, and the probable odds of our success are remote at best. Winning the lottery is luck.

Opportunity is not without risk, and it, too, has elements we cannot control. It should be a calculated risk based on reasonable assumptions. Opportunities can fail us, of course, but without a vision for opportunity, accumulating wealth is a very difficult proposition indeed.

By saying "I'd rather be lucky than smart," Dad taught me about opportunity—it just took me decades to understand the lesson. Dad was talking about risk and its potential. Financial gain does not come without placing a financial stake. I was in a place many times to profit but I lacked either the capital or the courage to act. Opportunity in the final analysis takes a great deal more than luck and intellect. It takes timing, courage, capital, and staying power. America is the land of opportunity for those who identify it and understand what it takes to benefit financially from it. Wealth is rarely created by random circumstance but rather, by a strong will, hard work, and the courage to assume risk.

OPPORTUNITY: Life is spontaneous. It cannot be controlled. Many times life will present more opportunities than we on our own could ever have created. To seize opportunity, we must be smart enough to recognize it and courageous enough to reach out and grab it.

The great end of life is not knowledge,
but action.

–Thomas Henry Huxley

Put Up or Shut Up

Inaction

*T*he rain was coming down outside, so Dad dragged out a deck of cards, and we started a game of penny-ante poker. Matches were our chips. It was a hot game; my three girls and I were playing with my dad, their "Honey." Nikki, my youngest, was barely old enough to play. But Nikki and Dad were skunking the rest of us. Dad always claimed Nikki had great card sense.

As it neared dinnertime, Dad dealt the last hand. Both Dad and Nikki were grinning ear to ear. Each of them thought they had the winning hand. Good sports Kristy and Suzy, my other two girls, stayed in the game with half-hearted bets and drew a few cards. As the turn to draw and bet rolled to Dad, he lowered his head till his eyes met Nikki's. He said, "I don't want any cards, and I'll bet it all and call you."

Nikki sat frozen. She looked at me as if to ask for help. I leaned over to look at her cards, and she had a great hand. We whispered back and forth as though real dollars were at stake, until Dad straightened and laughed as he said, "Well? Are you going to put up or shut up?" At that, before I could say a word, Nikki panicked and folded.

Dad skunked us all right, but that was not the end of it. As he squealed in delight and began to claim victory with his "I'm the champ and you're the chump" taunt he revealed the real surprise.

Dad had a bust hand all along. He was just bluffing! Nikki was so mad that she had fallen for a trick. She had the winning hand and let it go. "What did you do that for, Honey?" she pouted over her loss.

"Well, I did it cause I could. Now, did I beat you or did you beat yourself? Next time, little girl, you won't be so easy to trick. If you want to win at cards, you've got to evaluate what you have and play what you have been dealt. Life's the same way, girls. You can't just sit there like a deer frozen in the headlights. You've got to put up or shut up, and that is all there is to it."

Either you have the courage of your convictions or you don't. You can sure bet your boots someone somewhere is going to challenge them.

INACTION: Learn to trust your own thinking; you may have more going for you than you know. If the reason for your action is sound, don't let others intimidate you into inaction. If you don't play, you can't win.

Time is a waste of money.

–Oscar Wilde

He Who Hesitates Is Lost

Hesitation

"*P*ull your hook. Quick, quick, pull your hook!" Dad shouted from the back of the boat.

I was daydreaming, sitting on the bow of the boat with my feet hanging just above the murky McKinney Lake water. Startled, I quickly yanked the cork back out of the water with such force that the empty hook flew over my head and into the boat.

"Watch out, blubber puss, you're gonna hook me!" an angry voice cried.

"Don't call me that, Sammy Junior!" I shrieked back in response.

"Kids, kids, settle down up there. You're going to scare all the fish away with your yelling."

As Dad was talking, he picked up my hook and reached down into the minnow bucket. He rebaited my hook and tossed it over the side.

"Now stay alert, Suzie Q, because he who hesitates is lost.

You've got to learn to be patient in life. When the fish bite, you've got to be ready. If you aren't ready to take advantage of the opportunity at hand, you'll miss the fish again."

"Kids you sit, you watch, you patiently wait, and when opportunity presents itself in life, you've got to be ready. You could learn worse lessons than fishing. You can lose more than a bass by not being ready for an opportunity. That old bass isn't going to hang around waiting for you to wake up. You better make up your mind now that you want to pull him in. You have to know what you are going to do before he bites, so when he does bite, you're ready for him. When you're fishing, the one who hesitates loses. Don't let the fish of this world eat your lunch."

HESITATION: Opportunities come at a specific point in time. Without a timely response, things change and the opportunity is seized by others. Was Daddy teaching us to fish or to respond to life's opportunities?

Money talks . . .
but all mine ever says is good-bye.

–Unknown

Easy Come, Easy Go

Prudence

*A*s Sammy Junior and I ran across the hardwood dance floor of the Lemmon Lake Clubhouse, we could hear Dad, A. C. Dunn, Fred Lorenz, and J. J. Lemmon a hoot'n and a holler'n as they played an afternoon game of penny-ante poker. In the late '40s, there was no air-conditioning to give relief from the unrelenting afternoon sun. In the heat of the day, everyone would take shade inside, play games, and wait for the cool of the evening. Dad was passing time and having fun with a bunch of crusty old cutups.

As Sammy Junior and I approached the game, J. J. let out a loud howl, signifying a big win on his part. About the same time, Dad pushed away from the poker table, grinning from ear to ear, and said, "easy come, easy go."

It seems that up until the very last hand Dad had accumulated a nice profit on his original penny-ante stake. To make the game more fun, they were playing a final winner-take-all round. Dad had lost, but no matter. It was always the sport of the game that pleased Dad the most, not the win.

"Easy come, easy go" was Dad's favorite expression after losing a poker game. Sammy Junior and I had heard it many times before, and we would hear it many more times throughout the years.

Years later, while I was working as a financial consultant for Merrill Lynch, I realized that individuals had very diverse and very strong emotional views about money. As I reflected on these extremes, I realized that our attitude depends on how easily we believe money can be accumulated. Our individual views on money are greatly affected by our experiences.

There are three important and distinctly different lessons hidden in the simple phrase "easy come, easy go." The first lesson is that our experience dictates our attitude. If money is hard to come by, then there is a natural tendency to hang onto it. This attitude was one that sprang from the Depression era. If money comes easily, then we begin to believe that it will always be there, and we spend more freely. This was the attitude of the high-tech bubble in 2000. The fact is, the past does not equal the future. Be careful with your money, whether it is hard or easily won. Economic conditions can change very rapidly.

The second lesson applies to jobs. For most Americans, a job is their source of income. Jobs that require only minimal skills offer the least reward (pay) and the least job security (you are easily replaced). A job that is easy for you to qualify for will be just as easy for others to qualify for as your replacement, hence, "easy come, easy go." If you want job security, you must develop skills that are in demand and hard to duplicate. A doctor is one of society's highest paid hourly workers. Medical skills are time-consuming and difficult to master. Few people have the persistence to become a doctor. The supply is limited; the need is high. It is a well-known economic principle that supply and demand establish prices in a free market.

As you prepare for the job market, are you keeping an eye on this economic law?

Finally, the adage is a life-sobering warning. If you have a casual or cavalier attitude toward money, you may just find that your nest egg is gone, or severely depleted. Money can dwindle through mismanagement, unpredictable economic shifts, or an investment gone awry.

PRUDENCE: While accumulation is the first step to money mastery, the second step is to understand how emotions and the economy interact to affect your feelings of financial well-being. The circumstances of your life today do not dictate the circumstances of your life tomorrow.

One of the greatest myths about entrepreneurs
is that they are risk seekers.
All sane people want to avoid risk.

–William A. Sahlmann, *Harvard Business School*

Win Some, Lose Some

Learn from Losses

"**D**ad, did you win some money?"

I knew that Dad and a bunch of the fishermen were over at the clubhouse and had been playing seven-card stud. They weren't playing for matchsticks, and it wasn't penny-ante poker. They were betting dollar bills! It looked like big money to a twelve-year-old. When I left the clubhouse, there was a pile of one-dollar bills in the center of the table and eight players circled around a big poker table.

Dad laughed and said, "No, little girl. I don't play poker to make money anyway. I do it for entertainment. I never lose more than my entertainment is worth. You win some, and you lose some."

Dad continued, "Games are not for making money, but they can teach you when to bet the odds and when to not go against the odds. In that respect, they have some things in common with business and making money. When you gamble, you're going to win some and lose some. The first gambling rule is don't ever bet more than you are willing to lose. That is the same rule for investing and business. And if you're in the game, you are going to lose some! Just make sure you win more than you lose and you'll be okay."

Dad's definition of "you win some, and you lose some," continued to broaden over the ensuing years. At one time or another, I would hear Dad apply this phrase to money, business, investments, health, and marriage.

It was his way of saying ups and downs are just part of life. Dad knew that Sammy Junior and I needed to develop perspective to handle both the good times and the bad. He also knew that for us to learn to handle business decisions and investment decisions, we had to accept that some failures were inevitable.

Fear of failure is the reason most people don't succeed. Most of us stop before we get started, or we "lose some" and quit. Dad wanted us to know how to play the financial game of life and win. This adage was his way of teaching us that success is built on winning and losing. Over time, the wins outnumber the losses if we learn from our mistakes. If we hold onto fear of failure, then we never give ourselves a chance to learn and "win some."

Investing is a great example. We have to learn to lose gracefully but do not waste the lesson. Learn something in the process. There is no way to master your financial needs if you are afraid to lose. Some loss is inevitable in the world of investing. The effort to avoid risk is a naïve "mission impossible." Embrace favorable calculated risks. Do your due diligence. Avoid uncalculated risk—it is gambling. We must risk time, capital, or both to win. This is true in love, life, and finance.

Understanding risk in financial terms is sorely needed. Risk concepts can be taught and learned. We have neglected to teach these principles in our educational system. Many adults cling to the false belief that there are risk-free investments. Dad would have warned them otherwise. Nothing is risk free; even money markets have risks. The question is, do you know what the risks are, and are you hedged against being wrong? The more you know about risk and the better you are at evaluating risk, the fewer "blind" risks you will take. Our adult population has not been taught the various categories of risk or how to evaluate one against the other. Holding cash has its risks, just like holding gold or holding stocks. None of these alternatives are free from risk; they just represent different risks.

As hard as it is to accumulate extra cash, our culture encourages us to consume it rather than invest it. Investing takes a lot of personal discipline, especially when an investment does not work out. After a failed investment, our first thought is how much happier we would be if we had just bought that new car or new couch instead.

It is a sad fact that many people spend tens or hundreds of thousands of dollars for a college education only to find out that their major field of study has no economic value. Those students who spent their funds on education for which there is no economic demand have not invested their time or money for their economic benefit. These students have lost economic value; yet, no one would ever advocate that they should never learn anything again. Students go on learning from their mistakes. Some students go back and start over with a new course of study that can produce the economic rewards they are after.

Many students learn too late that they have used their college education much like a consumable commodity. You either consume market value or you create market value. Which type of education did you pursue?

Most of our society spends money and time on items that offer no economic return. In other words, they are consumers. They consume all the money they create, and they consume all the free time they have. It is like eating from a garden without ever replanting a crop.

The fullness of life is to embrace risks with clear forethought and learn from the inevitable mistakes of the past. Each of us will "win some and loose some."

Learn from Losses: Financial maturity is attained through evaluating risks and making prudent decisions where the potential for gain outweighs the potential for loss. There is always a potential for both. To take a risk position, the potential for gain must far exceed the potential for loss. Never, ever risk that which you cannot afford to lose. No matter how good the choice initially appears; you will have losses. Learn from the loss, so it isn't a total loss.

The only sure thing about luck is
that it will change.

–Bret Harte

High Water Raises All Boats

Up Market Cycles

*T*imes were good. Mom and Dad seemed very happy and carefree. I was coming in from school, and Mr. Roper, the carpenter Mom had hired, was pouring a huge concrete addition to our family room and tearing out the hall staircase for a more modern look. The activity around the Potter renovation was huge. As I entered the kitchen for an after-school snack, Mom was excited.

"Look what your dad won!" she said, as she pointed to a big box on the den floor. "It's a new TV." Mom just beamed with pride. "Your dad won this as Potts-Knaur's top salesman of the year. The other sales guys really never had a chance. Your dad always produces twice as much as anyone else. Even in bad times, your dad can sell ice to an Eskimo. People just love him."

Well, now I was curious! I figured Dad was good at what he did, but until then, I really had no idea just how good. "What is his secret, Mom?" I asked, now that the subject had been raised.

"Well, if you ask him, he'll just claim that he works hard and the economy is strong right now. You know your dad is big on studying political and business news. He says it gives him a better idea how to approach his customers. Dad likes to make sure he sees what's on the horizon. Dad says that when times are good, "high water raises all boats." He'll also tell you when times are bad that it is just like taking the water out of the bathtub. When the stopper comes out, all the boats, big and little, drop down to the bottom. He says the times are good right now. As a country, we are in 'high cotton.' When things are going good, people feel comfortable spending more. It is always easier to sell when things are prosperous."

"But, Mom," I protested, "that explains why he let you add on to the house, but it doesn't explain why he always seems to be the best salesman every month and always wins the prizes."

"Oh, that's simple, Suzie. Your dad is the best month after month because selling is more important to him than it is to the other salesmen. Your dad really cares about his customers. He doesn't just sell supplies; he really helps them. He helps them personally, as well as with their businesses. Your dad is real smart, and his customers seek his advice on all kinds of things. You'd be surprised."

As I left the kitchen with a peanut butter and jelly sandwich in my hand, I thought, "No, I really wouldn't be surprised, because I think Dad is real smart, too."

UP MARKET CYCLES: The economy affects revenue on a quantitative basis. Relative success is dependent on a qualitative basis. Don't confuse the two types of success. If you assume you are creating financial success, but it is the market that is the largest contributor to your financial well-being, then the market can take it away as fast as it delivered it. Try to quantify how much of your success you can retain in a bad economy.

When Depression Hits, There Is No Floor

Down Market Cycles

*D*ad has been dead over fifteen years now. When I was growing up, he would tell me, "when depression hits, there is no floor." Dad's words on the Depression always seemed to be a statement out of nowhere. I really was not sure what he thought he was telling me. I'm not sure he knew either, but he had seen the Great Depression as a teenager, and his assessment of its impact was that nothing retained value. Value eroded quickly, and just as you thought values had hit the floor, they eroded again, and then again. Even though he had seen many bear stock market cycles since the Depression, Dad wanted me to understand the difference and the real havoc a true depression can create.

It is now 2002, and we are in the midst of one of the worst bear markets since the great market crash of 1929. For many workers, it is life as usual. For investors, it feels like their worst nightmare. I wish today that I had remembered to heed Dad's warning more closely. It seems so clear now as the pain increases with each market leg down into negative territory and I watch the erosion. The conventional wisdom of buy and hold for the long term seems to be deeply in question. A drop of 30 percent precedes a drop of 60 percent only to be followed by another round of lost value. Some stocks have lost 80 to 95 percent of their prior valuations. Preservation of capital is the name of the game, and a market that revalues by the moment is the quickest place to see the wisdom of Daddy's warning.

Most of the damage seems to be confined to financial assets. Let us hope that the damage does not expand and erode other asset types as well. It seems that in a vicious recession, just as with a depression, when it hits there seems to be no floor and no place to hide.

Dad would have said, "I've got good news and I've got bad news. The good news is that in a great up business cycle you don't have to be too smart to make money. The bad news is that in a down cycle you have to be brilliant to keep from losing your shirt!"

DOWN MARKET CYCLES: If the economy is headed down, watch out as the ceiling falls to the floor. Making money is never a sure thing. If we could read the future with absolute clarity, then investing would be easy. We need to learn from our mistakes and move on to new opportunities. Just know that at some point the down economy will revive, the market will reverse, and new investment opportunities will be born.

I am fond of pigs.

Dogs look up to us.

Cats look down on us.

Pigs treat us as equals.

–Winston Churchill

Pigs Get Fat, Hogs Get Slaughtered

Gain and Greed

"**W**hen you get out in the world, little girl, you need to remember that pigs get fat, and hogs get slaughtered. I've seen more good business deals die because of greed than any other reason. I've always believed that it was better to have 1 percent of something than 100 percent of nothing."

Dad just handed over this advice to me, a teenage girl who didn't have the faintest notion what he was talking about.

I don't think he expected me to understand at the time. And he certainly never enlightened me with the reason for the warning. Perhaps it was that a deal of his had just gone south, and since he couldn't fix the current deal, he figured he would at least try to fix the judgment that his children would carry into the world.

Over thirty years passed before I could relate Dad's advice to my world. I was a stay-at-home mom until I hit forty, and it was at that point that I reentered the working world. This saying held a core truth that I saw over and over again, as I began to move into various financial fields.

I've seen home sellers try to squeeze too much out of their market valuation only to be forced by their unrealistic greed to later accept a below-market price.

I've seen the "hogs" wait too late to sell a stock hoping to squeeze out the last dollar of profit only to see the stock fall many points below an earlier sell opportunity. I've seen stock buyers wait too long for a lower buy price only to see the stock rebound higher. I've seen the greedy try to squeeze too much from dropping mortgage rates only to miss the window of opportunity to refinance.

A greedy person only seems satisfied after the opportunity has passed them by. Those with a "close enough" strategy seem to consistently capture a better deal. The hog continually raises the bar, each time seeking more. The mentality of the hog is that there must be more available because they want it, not because there actually is more. Hogs rarely see the intrinsic value of the deal at hand.

Greed just doesn't serve in any field. When man becomes a servant of his greed, in the end he loses all. The Enrons and Michael Milkens of this world prove the point. Daddy counseled me more than once that he would "rather have 1 percent of something than 100 percent of nothing." And isn't that another way to say the same thing?

GAIN AND GREED: Learn to deal wisely and with fairness, and you will get financially fat. Profits can be made, but the greedy approach to any market can blind you to the realities. The cost of greed and its partner, selfishness, are steep. A win-win with reasonable gain is a better and more profitable way to live.

I've been poor and I've been rich,
and believe me—rich is better.

–Sophie Tucker

Grinning All the Way to the Bank

Debt Freedom

$\mathcal{I}$t was getting late on Saturday, and I had been downtown all day shopping with one of my girlfriends. We rode the streetcar home. At the stop by the Vogue Theater, we split to go our separate ways. I walked the four blocks home alone, carrying my purchases. As I came in the front door, I could hear Dad and Mom laughing and talking. When my eyes adjusted to the change in light, I saw Jimmie and Johnny Oster, old friends of Mom and Dad's.

It had been years since I had seen the Osters. Jimmie and Johnny were dating when Mom and Dad were dating, and they had been friends forever. Jimmie and Mom were all dressed up. They looked elegant, just like movie stars. Mom didn't like alcohol or beer, so she was drinking a Coke, and I think Jimmie was, too. Johnny and Dad had that smelly Old Turkey bourbon and Coke.

As Dad would say, they were "feeling their juice."

Dad was so happy. I'd never seen him so happy. "What are you guys celebrating?" I asked.

Dad said, "We are going to go out dancing, and we are going to cut a rug tonight! We just paid off the mortgage on the house, and we are *celebrating*!"

"Why is that so special, Dad?" I was clueless.

"Little girl, the only thing better than saving money is getting completely out of debt. From now on, the only time I'm going down to Republic National Bank will be to put money in my account, not the banker's. There is no joy in giving all your hard earned money away to the bill collectors. But there is plenty of fun to be had by keeping some of it for yourself and your future. I always liked more in-come than out-go. Yes, sirree, from now on I'll be collecting interest, not paying it. And we'll be grinning all they way to the bank!"

DEBT FREEDOM: It is important to get rid of debt and accumulate assets for the future. It will lower your risk and give you more options with your income. Determining if mortgage debt should be eliminated *depends* on tax law, alternate uses of money, market interest rates, and personal circumstances.

Maybe you can't take it with you,
but where can you go without it?

–Pearl Bailey

You Can't Take It with You

Money

$\mathcal{A}$s frugal as Sam Potter was in his own personal spending, he was always generous with whatever Mom wanted. Dad definitely managed to save, and when he found himself participating in a large spending indulgence, usually for Mom, he would always say, "Well, you can't take it with you."

It was always funny when he said it because Dad didn't have a mass consumerism bone in his body. He wasn't interested in fancy suits, shoes, cars, or houses. He loved friends and fun, and he planted vegetable gardens. Dad was a man of simple wants. Mom on the other hand loved pretty clothes, hundreds of shoes, real perfume, fur coats, and diamonds.

Dad loved Mom, and he accepted her excesses. Mom needed shoes the same way Imelda Marcos did. So, whenever we heard the words "you can't take it with you," Sammy Junior and I knew Mom was at it again, and we just had to laugh because Dad did. He thought her indulgences were foolishness, but he didn't say so outright. As long as he felt Mom wasn't getting too far out of hand, he wanted her to have all the things she never had as a child.

The irony of this saying is that if you didn't know Dad, you would have thought these words of wisdom were a license to free-wheeling spending. Nothing could be further from the truth! To Dad, this saying was a rationalization. He rationalized that it was okay to *temporarily* take your eye off the ball every now and then. Dad's focus was to provide for today, while he saved for the future. Dad was saving to provide for that inevitable rainy day, as well as to provide for a sunny tomorrow.

Financial diversions always seemed to be for Mom or us kids. It wasn't unusual for Mom to buy a new dress and hang it unworn in her closet for months. That way, she explained, as though coaching her daughter in a dying art form, when Dad asked her if it was a new dress she could truthfully say, "no, I've had it a long time." I don't know if Dad really bought that story, but Mom was certainly sold on it.

Dad was not much on self-indulgence. He never wanted to take his money with him to the grave or even spend it on himself in this life. Dad just had a long-term plan to create a quality lifestyle that allowed a comfortable retirement for himself and Mom.

Dad did not think it was fair for parents to end up financially dependent on their children. In prior generations, the aged looked to their children to provide their care. Dad's philosophy was indicative of a changing society, and he embraced the changes that the new culture created.

Dad understood that money had a primary function—to provide a comfortable lifestyle. After providing for daily survival, money takes on a secondary role, another purpose. Excess money can provide a secondary benefit to a family. Saved money acts as a cushion in bad times. Extra money can assure the ability to withstand a period of unemployment, whether voluntary or self-imposed.

Buying the things we need, which is the main function of money, is very well understood by the average person. Money's ability to provide future protection is very important but rarely considered and implemented. Our consumer society seems to disregard this need. Our consumer focus is on elevating the quality of our current lifestyle. Elevated spending occurs at the cost of protecting the future, and saving is delayed for a later day.

Dad was practical. He expected to be the first to die, and he wanted to leave behind the funds to take care of Mom. He did not want her to worry. Saving money for her was his way of saying, "I love you." Dad was not much for words of emotion; he showed his love in deeds. He never wanted to take his money with him; he just wanted to leave some behind for those he loved.

MONEY: As hard as we work to earn a living, as much time as we spend to accumulate things, at death they have no value. Only the spirit has a lasting net worth. The material assets we accumulate are left to help those we care about.

Retirement can be a great
time if you can figure
out how to spend time
without spending money.

–E. C. McKenzie

Don't Touch the Goose
That Lays the Golden Eggs

Retirement

*T*he day after my dad died in 1986, I went into the safe-deposit box to figure out my mom's financial condition. In the safe-deposit box were some municipal bearer bonds, no longer issued, with a note in my father's handwriting admonishing both the opener and my mother with the saying in big bold letters, "DON"T TOUCH THE GOOSE THAT LAYS THE GOLDEN EGGS."

I cried as I stared at Dad's handwriting. It seemed to speak with his voice, as though I could hear him say it in my ear. Even after his death he was still trying to teach the lessons he had learned.

Dad had saved for a rainy day by paying himself first, decade after decade. He put his savings to work for himself and Mom twenty-four hours a day. This final admonition was to my less frugal mother, as well as to my brother and myself. The message was clear: DO NOT ever deplete the principal, use only the interest. Hence, my advice to you, if you are planning retirement is to listen to Daddy's wisdom. Your plan must allow you to live decade after decade on the cash flow (interest, dividends, rents, etc.) without using the principal. You may live longer than you think, and what will you do then?

I fear that many of the financial consultants today allow the retiree to begin a principal depletion to subsidize a lifestyle without sufficient warnings. Many retirement plans act on the assumption that the client will die at a normal life expectancy or shortly thereafter. The problem is that none of us knows how long we may live. One of the fastest-growing sectors of our population is the elderly over one-hundred years of age. Can you imagine outliving your children and outliving your savings? What do your grandchildren or great-grand-children do to prevent a burden that they never anticipated?

After the death of my dad, I was constantly worried about my mother's lack of financial understanding. Mom never really under-stood the lessons that Daddy knew and taught so well. In her era, women did not bother with such matters. What a dangerous practice that was!

Dad's final and most important lesson about money was the lesson of the goose that laid the golden eggs. Once you have worked hard and sacrificed consumption to accumulate assets, then do not throw away the effort on foolishness. Money is a tool that, if properly invested, can become the goose that provides for your retirement years.

RETIREMENT—THE FINAL LESSON: Review the simple concepts that my dad taught and then build the skills you need to implement each one. Build your goose by understanding the power of money. See Appendixes A–E.

- Learn to save early and often.
- Use prudence and self-reliance in developing your skill set.

- Collect interest instead of paying it.
- Master economic skills.
- Look for opportunity and make your own decisions.
- Control hesitation and fear.
- Value your own thoughts.
- Respect the effort that it takes to earn money.
- Learn to take evaluated risks, where the potential rewards justify it.
- Don't let greed cloud your vision.
- Talk does not create results, action does.
- Be thankful that you are an American, where the opportunity for financial abundance is around every corner.
- Use up business cycles for gain; avoid down business cycles and cut losses.
- When you err and lose, learn from the loss.
- Build yourself a goose and take care of it, and it will feed and clothe you with its golden eggs.

But above all else, remember money is not the source of inner happiness; it is just a tool to care for our physical needs. Till we meet again. Sweet memories from my daddy, a "Honey" to us all.

The further backward you look,
the further forward you can see.

–Winston Churchill, *British Prime Minister*

THE WISDOM ENDS:

A Eulogy and History

Sam "Honey" Potter, A Life Completed

Sam Potter

(called "Honey" by His Grandchildren and Friends)

February 21, 1911– January 29, 1986

His Eulogy

*T*here is not a passing of a soul from this world into the next in which the family and friends are not stricken with their loss and bereave their loved one. And, at that time, the goodness of that humanity is remembered fondly. Pain fills the void in the knowledge that that human life will not interact with yours again.

I write this now in tribute to my father because as I grew from childhood to adulthood, I became more and more aware of the special gifts inherent in my father. Honey was not a perfect man, but the shortcomings or faults that gave him his humanity were few. What was so special about Honey that makes his going from us so very difficult was his capacity for humor and his sincere affection for his fellow man.

Many people, including myself, merely go through the day, and as our lives unfold we have some days filled with fun and some filled with sorrow. But most of our days are filled with neither—they only go by in a "non-event." Honey was special because he never seemed to have a "non-event" day. He took each day and wrung from it all its humor and drew pleasure in its simplicity. He had the objectivity to laugh at himself and poke fun at those around him. Honey's humor was a gentle nudge at us all when we became too uptight with the daily frustrations of living. Daddy never let the events or anger rob him of enjoying the time at hand. A flat tire, an overturned boat, things ruined, broken, or spoiled did not bring anger and hostility to the surface in my dad—instead he would convert the irritation into the humor of the day. That capacity to manufacture fun from frustration, and joy from simple events, made Sam Potter a man from whom we could all learn. Daddy did not expect or demand much of his family or friends. He seemed to give us the gift of total acceptance. Whatever we were was good enough. Honey wanted us all to be the best we could be, but he never closed in and demanded anything. He gave broad tolerance to our imperfections, and he never tried to constrain our personalities.

As much as each of us enjoyed and were direct beneficiaries of these traits, somehow the ability to copy or incorporate them into our own personalities seems elusive. I have not yet been able to incorporate into my own life the zest for living that my father clearly showed me was there for the taking. But if there is a message from Honey to us all, and a meaning in his passing, it is most assuredly this—Enjoy the wonder of the day, look at yourself and each other with love and a tolerant eye, find laughter in yourself and your humanity. And the frustrations of the day are just that—the frustrations. They are not the day.

Suzanne Potter Short
February 1, 1986

(Written in less than ten minutes upon awakening the morning after Daddy died. Not a single word was changed. It was read as written by his oldest granddaughter, Kristina Kay Short. Honey was the name Kristy gave her grandfather; it not only stuck but spread among his own personal circle of friends. It was a name that fit the man.)

Historical Background–Sam Potter

Shortly after Dad was born on February 21, 1911, his father left. To my knowledge he never returned. At seventeen, Dad lost his mother to cancer. He assumed the responsibility for the large medical debt before he got out of high school. He worked three jobs to pay off the hospital and the doctors. He had a newspaper route and operated a switchboard for the YMCA and, later, added the job of shipping clerk for Potts-Knaur Leather Co.

At age eighteen, Dad witnessed the 1929 stock market crash, and he lived through the Great Depression. He struggled to make ends meet and pay off debts. He watched assets plummet and jobs disappear overnight. In later years, Dad would warn me, "when depression hits, there is no floor."

Dad married his longtime sweetheart and ballroom dancing partner, Pauline Gressett, on June 10, 1935. One evening in 1936, he got on the Potts-Knaur freight elevator with the owner, Mr. Potts. Dad begged Mr. Potts to give him a chance to sell leather goods for the company. Mr. Potts gave him that chance. Dad's new job would put him on the road traveling Texas and Oklahoma, calling on shoe repair shops. He worked as a loyal traveling salesman for well over thirty years. Dad started selling right after the worst depression in our history. Those years of meager means gave him a great appreciation for "saving for a rainy day." His drive and personality made Dad Mr. Potts' top-producing salesman for decades.

Mom was twenty-two and Dad was twenty-four when they married. To save money, they delayed having children for almost six years. Mom and Dad's deferral of marriage and family was not common! Women not married by twenty were considered "old maids." Dad possessed a different financial vision from the very beginning, and he had the discipline and focus to follow his vision. Dad believed the key to financial independence was to start early and accumulate a nest egg. He would later teach my brother and me his fundamental core belief, "Money is the only thing I know that will work for you twenty-four hours a day."

Early in the marriage, Dad helped to financially care for my mother's half sister, Gracie. The pattern of helping Mom's family extended to my grandmother, Ora Mae Gressett, and even to my great-grandmother, Annie Jones. Dad also became a financial lending resource for some of his customers when they had need or fell on hard times.

Mom worked at Kress' and W.T. Grant's in downtown Dallas. Mom brought her weekly paycheck home, and Dad would give her a small amount for spending and lunch money. Dad was on the road driving from town to town all week, and he would come home on Friday night and be out on the road again Monday at 3:00 A.M. He was home three weekends a month. One weekend he would make a longer run, up into Oklahoma. Dad sold leather goods to "bring home the bacon," and Mom took care of the house, the kids, and the rent property. Dad maintained this schedule until he turned fifty-five in 1966.

Mom and Dad had bought two small rent houses side by side in Dallas right before they married in 1935. The homes were small, each with two bedrooms and one bath. They were located in the Oak Cliff area of Dallas. Mom and Dad lived in one house and rented out the one next door.

Years later, Dad told me that Saturday, December 6, 1941, the day before Pearl Harbor, he went out and bought four new tires for his car and put them under his bed. He was "uncomfortable about what was going on in Europe." He figured if we went to war with Hitler, tires would be hard to find. Since Dad was a traveling sales-man, his livelihood depended on his car. The one thing a car could not do without was tires.

American involvement in World War II started the next morn-ing on Sunday, December 7, 1941, as the bombing of Pearl Harbor was announced over radios across America. Dad's financial instincts were correct; within a few weeks, the government was in control of rubber production, and tires were in short supply for the duration of the war.

Dad was classified as 4F and was not allowed to fight in the war. He was destined to sell materials for a critical industry in the war effort. He was providing shoe materials for soldiers and civilians. The war years brought many grueling hours of work and travel.

I was born shortly before the start of World War II, on April 22, 1941. Mom and Dad had waited long enough for a family; Mom was twenty-eight and Dad was thirty. My brother, Sam Potter Jr., was born two-and-a-half years later on November 11, 1943.

In 1949, at age thirty-seven, Dad bought Superior Wholesale Meat Market with his brother-in-law, George Peterman. Dad provided the capital from savings and cash flow from his sales career at Potts-Knaur; Uncle George ran the business. It wasn't long before Dad and Uncle George decided to go their own separate ways. He settled with Uncle George and put a twenty-seven-year-old butcher, A. C. Dunn, in charge of managing the market, while he was on the road.

A. C. and his wife, Hazel, more than ten years younger than Mom and Dad, would become lifelong friends. Hazel and A. C. knew that Dad was "just smart." Hazel would later say; "If Sam Potter tells you it is going to rain, you better go buy an umbrella!"

Dad had good old horse sense and the courage to follow his instincts. By 1966, at age fifty-five, Sam retired from selling on the road. Dad and A. C. ran the market together until 1971.

Dad had accumulated more than a million dollars in net worth, and he would live on investments and buy discounted real estate notes for cash flow. Sam Potter understood the promise of America. He was an ordinary man who developed extra-ordinary wisdom. He lived a life of rags-to-riches because he learned the lessons of how money rewards and how it penalizes. He believed that "America is the land of opportunity." Dad taught himself the lessons of wealth creation. He knew poverty as a child; he knew that having money had to be better.

Dad valued family, freedom, fun, and financial security. This book is about the wisdom that allowed Dad to accomplish his goals and transform a life of poverty into a life of prosperity. Had he lived longer, Dad could have been the poster child for *The Millionaire Next Door* by Thomas J. Stanley, Ph.D., and William D. Danko, Ph.D.

Samuel and Pauline Potter
June 10, 1985
—on their 50th Wedding Anniversary

But where can wisdom be found?
Where does it dwell?
Man does not comprehend its worth;
it cannot be found in the land of the living.

—Job 28:12 & 13

$\mathcal{A}$PPENDIX
Interesting Extras

BONUS LESSON: Appendix A was my dad's message. As I researched for the origins of Daddy's quotes, I found this. Nothing is new under the sun, and wisdom is as old as the ages. No one could have said it better than Ben Franklin decades before the Declaration of Independence was written. To go forward, sometimes it is useful to go backward.

Mickle = Scottish term for much

Twopence = Old British coin worth two pennies

Groat = Old British coin worth four pennies

s. = shilling, a coin worth 12 pence or 1/20th of a pound

l. = basic monetary unit of exchange in the United Kingdom

Appendix A

"HINTS for those that would be Rich"

Poor Richard's Almanack, 1737

The use of Money is all the Advantage there is in having Money. For 6 *l.* a Year, you may have Use of 100 *l.* if you are a Man of known Prudence And Honesty.

He that spends a Groat a day idly, spends idly above 6 *l.* a year, which is the Price of using 100 *l.*

He that wastes idly a Groat's worth of his Time per Day, one Day with another, wastes the Privilege of using 100 *l.* each Day.

He that idly loses 5 *s.* worth of time, loses 5 *s.* and might as prudently throw 5 *s.* in the River.

He that idly loses 5 *s.* not only loses that Sum, but all the Advantage that might be made by turning it in Dealing, which by the time that a young man becomes old, amounts to a comfortable Bag of Money.

Again, he that sells upon Credit, asks a Price for what he sells, equivalent to the Principal and Interest of his Money for the Time he is like to be kept out of it: therefore

He that buys upon Credit, pays Interest for what he buys.

And he that pays ready Money, might let that Money out to use: so that

He that possesses any Thing he has bought, pays Interest for the Use of it.

Consider then, when you are tempted to buy any unnecessary Housholdstuff, or any superfluous thing, whether you will be willing to pay Interest, and Interest upon Interest for it as long as you live; and more if it grows worse by using.

Yet, in buying Goods, 'tis best to pay ready Money, because,

He that sells upon Credit, expects to lose 5 per Cent. By bad Debt; therefore he charges, on all he sells upon Credit, an Advance that shall make up that Deficiency.

Those who pay for what they buy upon Credit, pay their share of this Advance.

He that pays ready Money, escapes or may escape that Charge.

A Penny sav'd is Twopence clear, A pin a day is a Groat a Year, Save & have. Every little makes a mickle.

Appendix B

Estimated Future Retirement Income and Investment Nest Egg

Inflation rate = 3%

Years	Factor	Example Assumptions
1	1.03	1. Retirement goal 25 years.
2	1.06	2. Assume 3% inflation. Rate will vary.
3	1.09	3. Income in today's dollars that will sustain you.
4	1.13	4. Multiply factor times your today's income figure.
5	1.16	5. Assume no social security in figures.
6	1.19	
7	1.23	
8	1.27	
9	1.30	
10	1.34	
11	1.38	
12	1.43	
13	1.47	
14	1.51	
15	1.56	
16	1.60	
17	1.65	
18	1.70	
19	1.75	
20	1.81	
21	1.86	
22	1.92	
23	1.97	**MATH FOR RETIREMENT NEST EGG TARGET**
24	2.03	
25	**2.09**	1. Today's income is $50,000 x 2.09 = $104,500
26	2.16	2. Income in tomorrow's dollars = $104,500
27	2.22	3. Nest egg calculation = $104,500 x 20
28	2.29	4. Retirement nest egg needed = $2,090,000
29	2.36	
30	2.43	
31	2.50	
32	2.58	
33	2.65	
34	2.73	
35	2.81	
36	2.90	
37	2.99	
38	3.07	
39	3.17	
40	3.26	

Appendix C

Power of Compounding over Long Periods of Time

Total Years	"A" Cumulative $$ Invested	+	"B" Total Interest $$$ Earned	=	"C" Year-end Value	
1	$1,200	+	$39	=	$1,239	
2	$2,400	+	$168	=	$2,568	
3	$3,600	+	$393	=	$3,993	
4	$4,800	+	$721	=	$5,521	
5	$6,000	+	$1,159	=	$7,159	
6	$7,200	+	$1,716	=	$8,916	
7	$8,400	+	$2,400	=	$10,800	
8	$9,600	+	$3,220	=	$12,820	
9	$10,800	+	$4,186	=	$14,986	
10	$12,000	+	$5,308	=	$17,308	
11	$13,200	+	$6,599	=	$19,799	
12	$14,400	+	$8,069	=	$22,469	
13	$15,600	+	$9,733	=	$25,333	
14	$16,800	+	$11,604	=	$28,404	
15	$18,000	+	$13,696	=	$31,696	
16	$19,200	+	$16,027	=	$35,227	
17	$20,400	+	$18,613	=	$39,013	
18	$21,600	+	$21,472	=	$43,072	
19	$22,800	+	$24,625	=	$47,425	B = A interest is working as hard as you
20	$24,000	+	$28,093	=	$52,093	
21	$25,200	+	$31,898	=	$57,098	
22	$26,400	+	$36,065	=	$62,465	
23	$27,600	+	$40,619	=	$68,219	
24	$28,800	+	$45,590	=	$74,390	
25	$30,000	+	$51,007	=	$81,007	
26	$31,200	+	$56,902	=	$88,102	
27	$32,400	+	$63,311	=	$95,711	
28	$33,600	+	$70,269	=	$103,869	B = 2A interest is working 2 times harder
29	$34,800	+	$77,817	=	$112,617	
30	$36,000	+	$85,997	=	$121,997	
31	$37,200	+	$94,855	=	$132,055	
32	$38,400	+	$104,441	=	$142,841	
33	$39,600	+	$114,806	=	$154,406	
34	$40,800	+	$126,008	=	$166,808	B = 3A interest is working 3 times harder
35	$42,000	+	$138,105	=	$180,105	
36	$43,200	+	$151,164	=	$194,364	
37	$44,400	+	$165,254	=	$209,654	
38	$45,600	+	$180,449	=	$226,049	B = 4A interest is working 4 times harder
39	$46,800	+	$196,830	=	$243,630	
40	$48,000	+	$214,480	=	$262,481	

Chart Assumptions

7%	= After-tax rate
$100	= Saves monthly $$
Monthly	= Compounds
"A"	= Your total $$
"B"	= Total interest
"C"	= Year-end value

THE POWER OF COMPOUNDING is that money starts to work and gradually the interest assumes more and more of the productive work. In 19 years, the interest is working as hard as you are at adding to your wealth. Add 9 more years, and it is working 2 times as hard. Add 6 more years, and it is doing 3 times the work. Add 4 more years, and it is doing 4 times the work. The power of compounding accelerates over time.

Appendix D: Graph Version of Appendix C

Power of Compounding over Long Periods of Time

Graph Appendix C.

   "A" • **Cumulative $$ Invested**: is the sum of your $100 per month times the number of months you contributed. (Example: end of 1ˢᵗ year is $1200 or $100 x 12 months.) It compounds monthly at an after-tax rate of 7%.

   "B" • **Total Interest $$$ Earned**: is the total interest cumulative through the year-end. It illustrates how much of the growth is from the compounding of interest. (Note: that by the 19th year in the example, the interest earned-to-date becomes larger than your personal contribution-to-date and the earnings relative to contribution gets stronger and more dominate over time.)

   "C" • **Year-End Value**: is the account at the end of the year, assuming it compounds monthly at an after-tax rate of 7%.(C is A+B.)

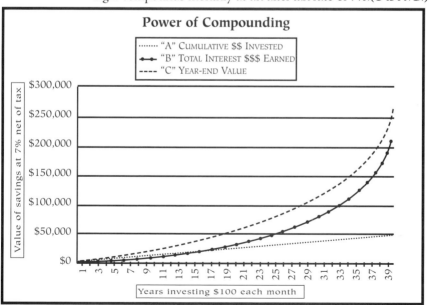

Appendix E
Why the Poor Get Poorer and the Rich Get Richer

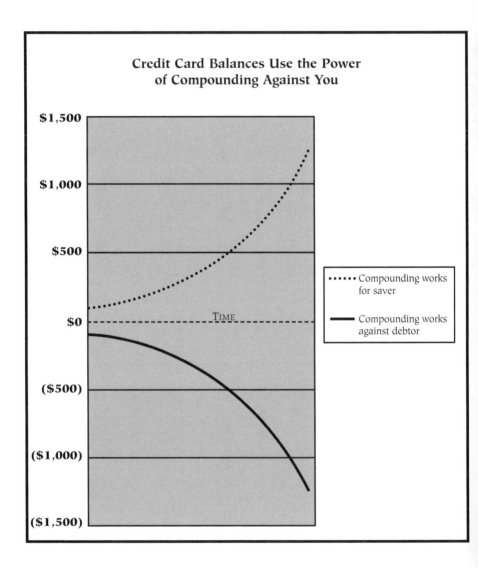

INDEX

Index of Lessons

BEHAVIOR: By repeating hurtful things, we set in motion injury to our   39
fellowman. None of us attain perfection in this world, so why find fault
in others? A person of character knows that there are enough faults needing remedy within ourselves to occupy us for a lifetime.

CAPITALISM: We all accept on some level that America is a country full   277
of opportunities, but very few of us understand that the financial limitations in our life are frequently self-imposed. Biographic evidence of
phenomenal success is prolific. Many financial success stories started
from a point of limited education and limited financial resources, but
they never involved limited determination.

CHILDREN AND JOY: Kids focus on the joy, not the job. Adults focus on   169
the job, not the joy. Who should be the teacher?

COMMITMENT: More valuable than a smart man, a rich man, and a   55
successful man is a man of integrity. Do what is right; say what you
mean; mean what you say.

DEBT FREEDOM: It is important to get rid of debt and accumulate assets   303
for the future. It will lower your risk and give you more options with your
income. Determining if mortgage debt should be eliminated *depends* on
tax law, alternate uses of money, market interest rates, and personal
circumstances.

DETERMINATION: Determination is the force that moves us forward. It   79
moves us over, under, around, and through the obstacles in life.

DISCIPLINE OF ACCUMULATION: If you don't pay yourself first, nobody   257
else will. The future arrives before you know it, and the time to start
planning is now.

DOWN MARKET CYCLES: If the economy is headed down, watch out as   299
the ceiling falls to the floor. Making money is never a sure thing. If we
could read the future with absolute clarity, then investing would be easy.
We need to learn from our mistakes and move on to new opportunities.
Just know that at some point the down economy will revive, the market
will reverse, and new investment opportunities will be born.

ENTITLEMENT: To make a lot of money you must put forth the energy to   239
make it happen.

Fun: Joy is where you find it and if you can't find fun in the day, make   173
some. Age does not have to rob anyone of childhood playfulness or
energy for living.

Gain and Greed: Learn to deal wisely and with fairness and you will   301
get financially fat. Profits can be made, but the greedy approach to any
market can blind you to the realities. The cost of greed and its partner,
selfishness, are steep. A win-win with reasonable gain is a better and
more profitable way to live.

Gift of Life: Take full advantage of every opportunity that life offers,   77
or the time to take advantage of that opportunity may pass you by.

Give and Take: Life isn't a zero-sum game. If you want to have a good   191
time, you have to be willing to give a good time. We must look for our
own joy, even when we feel others are beating us in the competitive
game of life.

Gratitude: The source of happiness is found in a sense of gratitude. No   127
matter what you have, there are those with less and those with more.

Guideline for Life: The second most important commandment given   9
by Jesus in the *New Testament* is: "Love your neighbor as yourself."
(Mark 12:31) All the lessons of character can be found in Scripture, and
the fundamental rule for living with your fellow man is the Golden Rule.

Happiness: Happiness is an emotional feeling produced by your atti-   203
tude toward life. Money is a medium of exchange, a thing, not a feeling.
Money cannot of itself make you happy or unhappy.

Hesitation: Opportunities come at a specific point in time. Without a   287
timely response, things change and the opportunity is seized by
others. Was Daddy teaching us to fish or to respond to life's opportunities?

Honesty: Be honest in all things. Honesty is so essential to defining   49
character that it becomes unthinkable to value any achievement that
lacks it. "Whoever can be trusted with very little can also be trusted with
much, and whoever is dishonest with very little will also be dishonest
with much." Luke 16:10

Humor: Life delivers the unexpected. Our attitude determines how we   195
experience it. Cultivate an attitude that creates fun and pleasure out of
"bad luck."

LUCK AND PERSISTENCE: The most direct route to achievement is to do 113 what others aren't willing to do. At times, it may be the only route. Achievement isn't a matter of luck; it is a matter of persistence.

MAXIMIZING RETURN: The early bird proverb is true in building a retire- 235 ment fund, in growing a business, and in advancing a career.

MISERY: In what pattern of behavior are we engaged? Approach life's 149 pains with caution. If we focus all our energy on these, we miss the positives life offers. Until we focus attention toward the positives, we cannot and will not develop a plan to move on.

MONEY: As hard as we work to earn a living, as much time as we spend 305 to accumulate things, at death they have no value. Only the spirit has a lasting net worth. The material assets we accumulate are left to help those we care about.

MONEY FOLLOWS VALUE: The way to make more money is to create 255 more value. Money follows value, not the other way around.

MONEY'S POWER: It takes money to survive. You can work till you die, or 223 you can find something or someone else to work for you. If you own investments that can generate as much money as you need for personal survival, then, and only then, have you achieved financial independence. How can you get those investments? It all starts with the commitment to save money specifically for investing.

NEGATIVE POWER: Action is the child of a belief. Result is the child of 111 action. No belief, no action, no results. "If you can't you must." Anthony Robbins.

OPPORTUNITY: Life is spontaneous. It cannot be controlled. Many times 281 life will present more opportunities than we on our own could ever have created. To seize opportunity, we must be smart enough to recognize it and courageous enough to reach out and grab it.

PAIN: Time dulls all pain and fades all pleasure. The promise of tomor- 145 row will eventually outweigh the pain of yesterday.

PATIENCE: It takes time plus patience to build a better you. 73

PERSPECTIVE: Life is a precious gift, and we need to be grateful and 137 appreciate fully each day as it is given.

Sometimes, we need to change our strategy and approach a situation from a new perspective.

RETIREMENT: Review the simple concepts that my dad taught and then   309
build the skills you need to implement each one. Build your goose by
understanding the power of money.

- Learn to save early and often.
- Use prudence and self-reliance in developing your skill set.
- Collect interest instead of paying it.
- Master economic skills.
- Look for opportunity and make your own decisions.
- Control hesitation and fear.
- Value your own thoughts.
- Respect the effort that it takes to earn money.
- Learn to take evaluated risks, where the potential rewards justify it.
- Don't let greed cloud your vision.
- Talk does not create results, action does.
- Be thankful that you are an American, where the opportunity for
  financial
  abundance is around every corner.
- Use up business cycles for gain; avoid down business cycles and
  cut losses.
- When you err and lose, learn from the loss.
- Build yourself a goose and take care of it, and it will feed and clothe
  you with its golden eggs.

But above all else, remember money is not the source of inner happiness; it is just a tool to care for our physical needs.

RISK AND REWARD: Rewards are rarely found in the safe decision.   271
Rewards are found in assuming calculated risks, both personally and
financially.

RULES: Character is both taught and developed. If children have been   29
taught what is right, as they begin to accept the rules, then all that has
to be done or said is to remind them that they know what to do and they
need to just do it. If children are not taught correct behavior, it is folly to
believe that a child will learn it independently. "Train a child in the way
he should go, and when he is old he will not turn from it." Proverbs 22:6

SAVING: Understand the difference in the value of pretax and posttax   211
money. Never assume small quantities of money saved over time won't
create value. It is faulty thinking.

TIMING: There are some events in life that later is too late and now is too 265 soon. Get the timing right; it is crucial.

TRUTH: Character is not built or maintained with bold giant steps, but by 53 resisting the small temptations. Truth is its own beauty. A distortion of the truth inevitably springs its own trap.

UP MARKET CYCLES: The economy affects revenue on a quantitative basis. 297 Relative success is dependent on a qualitative basis. Don't confuse the two types of success. If you assume you are creating financial success, but it is the market that is the largest contributor to your financial well-being, then the market can take it away as fast as it delivered it. Try to quantify how much of your success you can retain in a bad economy.

VALUE OF FAMILY: The market place may value our time in dollars, but 153 love and family are not measured in the market place; they are weighed in the heart. In life's hierarchy, human relationships are the greater wealth.

VALUE OF THOUGHT: Our thoughts are our greatest source of value. 27 Every created thing that is was a thought before it was a thing.

VALUE OF YOU: There are many things in life more valuable than assets. 121 In *this world* health, happiness, friends, and most of all family, are priceless. Things are just that—things. Part of character is the art of understanding what matters most. ". . . a man's life does not consist in the abundance of his possessions." Luke12:15

VERBAL RESPONSIBILITY: Words are powerful and should be selected 35 with care. Words can cause both pain and pleasure. The spoken word has a lifespan long beyond the moment. Weigh your words with care. We need to be prudent with our words, eager to praise and slow to blame.

VIEWPOINT AND TOLERANCE: It is human to view life in our own unique 23 way. Because of that, we place our own individual interpretation on what we see and hear. The strength of our country is that, as Americans, we have the right to hold our own points of view. In this free nation, each man has the right to draw different conclusions from the same information. There is beauty in the tolerance of different viewpoints. Two people of different views can both have character. It is not the same perspective that creates character, but how we handle our own point of view.

About the Author
Suzanne Short

$\mathcal{S}$uzanne Short encourages women to become more financially savvy and to take control of their destinies. Suzanne's successful careers as a Realtor, stockbroker, and morgage broker give her a broad financial background. A much-sought-after speaker, she is busy writing her next book, tentatively titled, *Wisdom Daddy Taught Me for Kids*. She and her husband reside in Irving, Texas.

Suzanne says, "If, as many Americans, you are in need of credit repair and financial coaching, please visit my web site for additional tips.

BOOKS AND AUDIOS AT
WWW.SHORTCONCEPTS.COM
WWW.BROWNBOOKS.COM
OR TOLL FREE 866.WISDOM.4

Suzanne's Mission Statement

I, Suzanne Short, know, feel, and believe that my life's purpose is to use the gifts I was given as an engine moving forward, not just a vessel, passively containing those gifts.

I will grow to new levels of self-fulfillment so that I have the expanded abilities to help myself and others live empowering lives without fear.

I will seek and do God's will in my life and work for the financial, spiritual, emotional, and physical welfare of not only myself, but also of my loved ones, my friends, my acquaintances, and my world.

I have shared Honey with you; now please share *Wisdom Daddy Taught Me* with a friend.

	DATE DUE		
1/40/07			